AppSec in a Nutshell

A Brief Intro into Application Security

Martian

Book production by CyberScribe Press LLC
Formatting and Editing by MysticqueRose Publishing

ISBN: 979-8-9907209-0-9

Martian

Printed Worldwide
First Printing 2025
First Edition 2025

Dedication

To my sister Aaliyah whose light was extinguished far too soon.

This book is a tribute to your spirit, a reminder that love endures and that justice, in its own way, will find its path.

You are forever in my heart.

Purpose and Audience

This book is intended to offer a high-level understanding of the various technologies and best practices that can be implemented to secure applications and prevent attacks.

The following groups of people may find this book especially useful:

- Intermediate-level security professionals: This book is for those who are new to the field of application security, as well as those who have some experience but are looking to expand their knowledge and skills. This book may not be a fit for someone that is not already well-versed in some basic cybersecurity principles.

- Penetration testers: Pentesters looking to improve their skills in identifying and reporting vulnerabilities in software will find this book useful.

- Developers: Developers will learn about common vulnerabilities, secure coding practices, and how to test their applications for security vulnerabilities.

- Bug bounty hunters: Individuals who are interested in bug bounty programs will learn about the best practices for identifying and reporting vulnerabilities in a bug bounty context.

- Managers and stakeholders: Managers and other stakeholders who are responsible for the security of web applications will learn about the importance of application security testing, regulatory requirements, bug bounty programs, and have a basic understanding of these programs.

Table of Contents

Introduction

As cyber threats continue to develop and multiply, developers and security professionals face significant challenges in their initiatives to protect applications and sensitive information.

This book provides a general understanding of these technologies and best practices, and it is a valuable resource for developers, security professionals, and anyone looking to improve their understanding of application security.

By completion of this book you will gain the expertise and foundational knowledge needed to take on the challenges of the software development lifecycle and modern application security, enhancing your ability to protect digital assets in a dynamic security environment.

Understanding AppSec

What Is AppSec?

Applications are the face of businesses today. Whether you are a small business or a large conglomerate, having an online presence is almost mandatory to stay ahead. Enormous power also comes with great responsibility, and since applications are the face of businesses, they also become a prime target for cyberattacks.

An application can easily be compromised if proper security measures are not considered during development and testing. This is where application security testing comes into play. Application security can occur in several stages, but establishing best practices is most often done in the application development phases. However, companies can also take advantage of different post-development tools and services. Hundreds of security tools are available to businesses, each serving unique purposes. Some enforce code changes, others monitor code for threats, and others establish data encryption. Additionally, companies can choose more specialized tools for different types of applications.

Applications are often the target of cyberattacks. According to Symantec's study, 43% of all attacks are directed at small businesses. Hackers can attack your applications for any number of reasons. They could be trying to steal sensitive data, such as customer information or financial data. They might also be looking to take down your application for political reasons or to wreak havoc.

It is essential to ensure that your applications are safe from these attacks; whether due to a technical error or an intentional attack, it is something that every company must address.

What's included in the concept of Application Security?

Processes, technologies, and practices make up the discipline of application security. These protect applications from threats throughout the application lifecycle. Cybercriminals are organized, specialized, and motivated to detect and exploit vulnerabilities in business applications to steal data, intellectual property, and sensitive information. Application security can help organizations protect all applications (such as legacy systems, desktops, and microservices) used by internal and external stakeholders, including customers, business partners and employees.

What is OWASP?

An online community called the **Open Web Application Security Project** creates openly downloadable tools, technologies, approaches, and articles on web application security. The OWASP offers open, free resources, and the OWASP Foundation, a non-profit organization, runs it. Local chapters, conferences, and a handful of open-source software development programs and toolkits are just a few of their projects.

A decent starting point for writing secure programming is the OWASP Top 10. A scan of 130,000 applications for our State of Software Security Volume 11 revealed that roughly 68% had security vulnerabilities in the OWASP Top 10.

The OWASP Top 10 is more than simply a ranking. It rates the risks associated with each error category using the OWASP Overall Risk methodology and offers recommendations, case studies, examples, and references for each risk. Application developers can take actionable measures toward building a more secure application by learning about the problems listed on the OWASP Top 10 chart and how to fix them. This will help protect users from harmful cyberattacks. Of course, OWASP's list of vulnerabilities/risks is one of many things developers should be aware of.

OWASP TOP 10 Risks for Web Apps

According to OWASP, what are the top 10 risks? This list of vulnerability categories is from OWASP Top 10 2021, which is current at the time of writing this book (OWASP Top 10 2025 is also in draft, ensure to review latest when available):

1. Broken Access Control

Attackers can quickly grab whatever they want if authentication and access restrictions are not built correctly. Users who aren't authorized or authenticated may have access to sensitive data and systems or even privilege settings if control is breached.

Since automated systems can't always test for them, configuration mismatches and insecure access control procedures can be challenging to spot. Although penetration testing can identify missing authentication, different techniques are required to identify configuration issues. Safe coding techniques can help to prevent lax access controls and problems with password management, as can preventive approaches like locking down administrative accounts and controls and introducing multi-factor authentication.

2. Cryptographic Failures

Cryptographic failures pertain to vulnerabilities within cryptographic systems that may result in data breaches or compromise of systems. This is related to the protection of data both in transit and at rest, including the use of weak cryptographic algorithms, inadequate key management, and the failure to encrypt sensitive information. To protect against these vulnerabilities, it is important to use strong encryption algorithms, adopt effective key management strategies, and ensure the security of data during transmission and storage. Organizations should categorize the data processed, stored, or transmitted by their applications and ascertain which data qualifies as sensitive under applicable privacy laws and regulatory standards.

3. Injection

Injection occurs when attackers exploit insecure code to insert (or inject) their code into a program. Attackers can use injection attacks to access secure areas and essential information by impersonating authorized users since the program cannot detect code inserted in this way from its code. Examples of injections include SQL injections, command injections, CRLF injections, and LDAP injections.

Testing for application security can identify injection problems and suggest fixes, including filtering special characters from user input or creating parameterized SQL queries.

4. Insecure Design

This risk highlights how important it is to follow secure design principles when creating software. More specifically, Insecure Design is about the flaws in design and architecture that can create weaknesses in applications. To tackle this issue, weave security into every part of the development process, use secure design patterns, and apply threat modeling during the design stage. Providing regular security training for developers and conducting detailed code reviews can also boost the security of the application's design.

5. Security Misconfiguration

Security misconfiguration arises from improperly configured security controls, default settings, or incomplete configurations across any level of an application stack. This can include network services, web servers, application servers, databases, and more. More general security configuration problems provide significant dangers that enable attackers to easily access sensitive data and site areas, similar to improperly configured access controls.

6. Vulnerable and Outdated Components

Using vulnerable and outdated components can make applications susceptible to various attacks because of known weaknesses in third-party libraries or frameworks that haven't been updated or patched. Keep a list of all components used in applications, ensure they are regularly updated to the latest versions, and create a strong software update policy to avoid running into this issue. Employing software composition analysis (SCA) tools can effectively identify vulnerable components.

7. Identification and Authentication Failures

A severe security risk might arise from improperly implemented authentication and session control operations. These issues make it simple for attackers to take the identities of legal users.

For example, if a user account on a forum allows easy password recovery without proper verification, it could be exploited by attackers. Implementing multi-factor authentication and enforcing strong password policies can significantly enhance security. Even before the code is deployed, use DAST and SCA scans to find and fix errors with implementation problems.

8. Software and Data Integrity Failures

This risk comes from trusting that software updates or data are safe without checking them first. Picture downloading what looks like a normal software update, but it actually has malware because it wasn't verified. To avoid this risk, always check the integrity of software updates with checksums or digital signatures.

9. Using Security Logging and Monitoring Failures

Security logging and monitoring failures highlight the dangers of insufficient logging and monitoring that can lead to undetected breaches over time. Without proper logging practices in place, organizations may struggle to detect incidents promptly or conduct effective forensic investigations after a breach occurs. Poor monitoring systems, failure to record problems or assaults, and human error can heighten security problems. For instance, if a personal website does not log failed login attempts, an attacker could repeatedly try passwords without being noticed. Implementing comprehensive logging practices and regularly reviewing logs can help detect suspicious activities early. Threat actors design their assaults to take place before you can observe or respond by taking advantage of the need for reasonable adjustments and lengthier remediation timeframes.

To address this risk, organizations should implement comprehensive logging practices across all systems, utilize security information and event management (SIEM) systems for real-time alerting on suspicious activities, and establish incident response procedures.

10. Server-Side Request Forgery

SSRF happens when an application retrieves a remote resource without properly checking the URL provided by the user. For example, if a web app lets users submit URLs to fetch images without any validation, a hacker could misuse this to access internal services. To reduce SSRF risks, make sure to implement strict checks for URLs and use allowlists for accessing remote resources.

Other Common Application Vulnerability Considerations

➢ Binary Protection

Jailbreak/Poor Root Detection: When a device gets rooted or jailbroken, the OS' data security and encryption features are removed. When a device is compromised, malicious code may be run, and the intended behavior of the application logic may be drastically altered. On rooted devices, recovery and data forensic programs frequently function as planned, and accurate root/jailbreak identification is required to keep the data from being revealed.

➢ Insufficient Authorization/Authentication

Authentication is the process that software developers use to make sure that only the right people can access an application. It verifies that a user is who they claim to be. This is typically done by asking for a username and password when someone tries to log in. Multi-factor authentication takes it a step further by requiring more than one way to prove identity. This could involve something you know (like a password), something you have (like your phone), and something you are (like your fingerprint or face).

Authorization comes into play after a user has been authenticated. Once a user is confirmed, the system checks if they have permission to use the application. It does this by matching the user's identity against a list of people who are allowed access. It's important that authentication happens first, so the application only checks the credentials of users who have been verified against the authorized user list.

- **Insecure storage of information**

  Insecure storage of sensitive data in the device may lead to vulnerability. It's essential for people to remember that data saved on gadgets isn't secure because it might be stolen, and sensitive data stored on the device could also be stolen. To avoid this risk, apps should maintain sensitive data in keychain pairs, and the data must be encrypted if the app stores data in the form of data.

- **Server-Side Vulnerability**

  Unauthenticated access can be prevented on the server side, but app design must incorporate input validation checks and limits to reduce the server's effort. Verifying input data and halting any odd behavior is critical when the app processes the server. The relevant data types can be safely listed, and the remainder can be blocked from the app side. The server and the app should employ encryption when transferring and receiving data.

➢ Insecure Source Code

We know that the first entry points into an application are faults and vulnerabilities in the code. Attackers are repacking to reverse your code and need to give your logic a chance to win. They would use a public version of your software to alter the current situation. In this scenario, you can make a replica of your source code and store it for future use in maintenance. A developer can think of a Code Signing certificate, which provides program code and high security to safeguard principles. The code has remained the same since it was signed, and the certification authenticates it. Additionally, it confirms the authenticity of the publisher. Several inexpensive SSL service providers in the SSL industry can guarantee the integrity of the application code.

➢ Cryptography - Improper Certificate Validation

The app can validate SSL/TLS certificates, or it won't; it might need to verify the state correctly. The client may sever the connection if the cert cannot be verified. If the data is not properly vetted, it may be utilized for unlawful access. To confirm whether a certificate is from a reliable source and should come from a renowned certificate authority, you must make sure the certificate validation in your app is carried out correctly. Including any modern standard forums for the best validation would be best.

➢ Insufficient Session Expiration

The identifiers get invalidated when a user logs out of the program. Even then, other users may still interrupt and act on behalf of the users if the server crashes to invalidate the session identifiers. You must check the program's logout button and wait for a proper logout before the session is appropriately invalidated. The key is to download apps responsibly and with common sense. We can only hope your future apps contain fewer of these vulnerabilities in mobile applications.

Application Security Trends Today

Application security is a quickly evolving field, with new threats and vulnerabilities emerging regularly. Organizations are facing several challenges in securing their applications, such as:

- **The shift towards cloud-based and mobile applications:** These applications are often distributed and accessed from multiple locations and devices, making it more difficult to secure them and protect them against threats such as data breaches, unauthorized access, and malicious insiders. Cloud and mobile applications can introduce new vulnerabilities and attack vectors, such as insecure data storage, lack of proper access controls, and the use of third-party services that may not meet the same security standards as the organization's own services.
- **The increasing use of open-source software and third-party components:** This can introduce vulnerabilities and potential attack vectors into an application, increasing the risk of a security breach. Open-source software and third-party components can contain known vulnerabilities, and organizations may not be aware of these vulnerabilities or may not have the resources to fix them. Additionally, organizations may need complete visibility into the code of third-party components, making it challenging to identify and mitigate vulnerabilities.
- **The rise of the Internet of Things (IoT):** With more devices being connected to the internet, organizations face new security challenges as many of these devices have limited security capabilities. IoT devices often have weak or hardcoded credentials, lack software updates and are easily exploitable. The lack of security

on IoT devices can also lead to attackers compromising the entire network and potentially accessing sensitive data and systems.

- **The increasing sophistication of cyber attackers**: Cyber attackers are continually developing new methods to exploit vulnerabilities and gain unauthorized access to sensitive data and systems. They are using more advanced techniques such as social engineering, phishing, malware and AI technologies to target organizations, and are also using automation and machine learning to scale their attacks. To address these challenges, organizations are turning to various security testing and bug bounty programs, as well as implementing secure coding practices and using security tools and frameworks. However, despite these efforts, many organizations are still unprepared to protect against the latest threats and vulnerabilities.

Organizations face various challenges in securing their applications as technology advances. To mitigate these risks, organizations must take a proactive approach to security. Additionally, they can implement the use of security testing, secure coding practices, security tools bug bounty programs and frameworks.

To build upon these proactive security measures, a major step in strengthening an organization's defense is to identify potential threats early in the development process. This is where threat modeling comes into play—a systematic approach to uncovering and addressing security risks before they can be exploited. By analyzing potential attack vectors and understanding how adversaries might target your system, you can design more resilient applications from the start.

Threat Modeling

At its core, threat modeling is a collaborative exercise that involves multiple stakeholders, including developers, security professionals, and business analysts. It is typically conducted at the design stage of a project but can also be done throughout the development lifecycle as new threats emerge.

Threat modeling typically involves four key steps:

1. **Identify assets:** The first step in threat modeling is identifying the assets that need protection. This might include sensitive data, intellectual property, or other resources that are critical to the operation of the system or application.

2. **Identify threats:** Once the assets have been identified, the next step is identifying potential threats that could compromise their security. This might include external attackers, insiders with malicious intent, or other sources of risk.

3. **Assess risks:** Once the threats have been identified, the next step is to assess each threat's likelihood and potential impact. This involves evaluating the probability of a threat occurring and the potential impact on the organization if it does.

4. **Mitigate risks:** Threat modeling aims to design and implement adequate security controls to mitigate the identified risks. This might include encryption, access controls, or other measures designed to prevent or minimize the impact of a security breach.

In order to detect and reduce potential security threats in software systems or other complex systems, threat modeling is a structured technique. The scope of the threat modeling exercise will depend on the specific system being modeled and the objectives of the practice.

Scope and Objectives of Threat Modeling

The scope of the threat modeling exercise should include a clear definition of the boundaries of the system being modeled, as well as the data flows and components that are critical to the system's security. This may include data inputs, processing logic, outputs, and external systems or networks interacting with the system.

The objectives of the threat modeling exercise should be defined based on the organization's specific security goals and priorities. For example, the objectives may include identifying and mitigating potential security risks in a particular application of software or system or assessing the overall security posture of the organization's IT infrastructure.

One key objective of threat modeling is identifying potential threats and vulnerabilities in the system. This may include technical vulnerabilities, such as unpatched software or weak authentication controls, and human factors, such as social engineering attacks or insider threats.

Another goal of threat modeling is to design and implement appropriate security procedures to reduce the risks identified. Technical safeguards like firewalls or encryption and rules and regulations for user conduct and access control may be included.

Overall, the scope and objectives of threat modeling should be defined based on the organization's specific security needs and priorities. By systematically assessing potential threats and implementing appropriate controls, threat modeling can help to reduce the risk of security breaches, data loss, and other security incidents that could have serious consequences for the organization.

Threat Modeling for AppSec

Threat modeling provides a structured approach to identifying potential security threats and vulnerabilities in an application, allowing developers to design and implement effective security controls to mitigate these risks.

1. **Identifying potential security threats and vulnerabilities:** Threat modeling allows developers to identify potential security threats and vulnerabilities in an application, both at the design stage and during the development lifecycle. By identifying potential security risks early in the development process, developers can take proactive measures to mitigate these risks and prevent security breaches.

2. **Improving security posture:** By identifying and addressing potential security threats and vulnerabilities, threat modeling helps improve an application's overall security posture. This can help reduce the risk of data breaches, cyberattacks, and other security incidents that could seriously affect an organization.

3. **Cost-effective security measures:** Threat modeling allows developers to identify the most cost-effective security measures to implement. By focusing on the most critical security risks, developers can prioritize their efforts and resources to ensure that the essential security threats are addressed first.

4. **Compliance with regulations and standards:** Many industries and regulatory bodies require compliance with specific security standards and regulations. By incorporating threat modeling into the development process, developers can ensure that their applications meet these requirements and avoid potential legal and financial penalties.

5. **Continuous improvement:** Threat modeling should be a constant process integrated into the development lifecycle rather than a one-time occurrence. By continually evaluating and improving the security of an application, developers can ensure that their applications remain secure in the face of new and emerging threats.

Threat Modeling provides:

- A structured approach to identifying potential security threats and vulnerabilities.
- Improving the security posture of an application.
- Ensuring compliance with industry standards and regulations.

By incorporating threat modeling into the development process, developers can design and implement effective security controls that mitigate potential security risks and prevent security breaches. APIs, databases, and other elements critical to the system's security. These components are then evaluated for potential threats and risks, such as vulnerabilities in the software or configuration errors.

Appropriate security controls are designed and implemented based on the identified threats and risks. These controls include technical measures such as firewalls, encryption, access controls, and policies and procedures to govern user behavior and access control.

The model's outputs might include a report or documentation outlining the identified threats and risks, the security controls that have been implemented, and recommendations for further improvements to the system's security posture.

Identifying Threats

Identifying potential attackers is an essential step in the threat modeling process. By understanding who might be motivated to attack a system, we can better anticipate the threats that are likely most relevant and design appropriate security measures to mitigate them.

Several types of potential attackers should be considered when conducting a threat modeling exercise. These include:

1. **Hackers:** External attackers motivated by financial gain, political agendas, or personal satisfaction. They may use various techniques, such as social engineering, phishing attacks, or brute force attacks, to gain unauthorized access to a system.

2. **Insiders:** Employees, contractors, or other individuals with legitimate access to a system but who may abuse their privileges for malicious purposes. Insiders may be motivated by financial gain, revenge, or personal gain.

3. **Competitors:** Other organizations or individuals seeking a competitive advantage by stealing intellectual property, customer data, or other sensitive information.

4. **Nation-states:** Governments or state-sponsored entities that may be motivated to target a system for political or strategic reasons. Nation-states may have access to sophisticated attack tools and techniques and may be willing to invest significant resources in targeting a system.

5. **Activists:** Individuals or groups who are motivated by social or political causes and who may seek to disrupt or damage a system to achieve their goals.

When identifying potential attackers, it is best to consider their motivations, capabilities, and likely attack vectors. For example, an external hacker might be more likely to use a remote exploit to access a system, while an insider might use their legitimate credentials to access sensitive data.

By considering the potential attackers who might target a system, we can better anticipate the threats that are likely most relevant and design appropriate security measures to mitigate them. This can help reduce the risk of security breaches, data loss, and other security incidents that could seriously affect an organization.

Benefits of Threat Modeling

Threat modeling is a critical component of the software development lifecycle. It involves identifying potential security threats and vulnerabilities in a system or application and implementing appropriate security measures to mitigate them. Threat modeling provides numerous benefits to businesses, including technical and business benefits.

Technical Benefits

1. **Early Identification of Security Risks:** Threat modeling allows businesses to identify potential security risks early in development. This makes it possible for companies to put in place suitable security measures before the system goes live, lowering the chance of data breaches and other potential vulnerabilities.

2. **More Effective Security Measures:** Businesses can implement more effective security measures by identifying potential security risks early in development. This can include implementing access controls, firewalls, and other security measures to protect against known threats.

3. **Better Risk Assessment:** Threat modeling allows businesses to conduct a more comprehensive risk assessment. This can help businesses to prioritize security risks and allocate resources more effectively to mitigate those risks.

4. **Reduced Security Costs:** Implementing appropriate security measures during development can be significantly cheaper than addressing security issues after the system is in production. Threat modeling can help businesses identify potential security risks early in the development process, reducing the cost of implementing security measures.

5. **Improved Collaboration:** Threat modeling is a collaborative process that involves various stakeholders, including developers, security professionals, and business leaders. By bringing together different perspectives, businesses can identify security risks more effectively and implement appropriate security measures. This can lead to improved collaboration and better communication between other teams and departments within the organization.

Business Benefits

1. **Improved Customer Trust:** Customers' anxieties about their data security are escalating in today's digital age. Implementing robust security measures can help businesses to build trust with their customers and protect their reputations.

2. **Competitive Advantage:** Businesses can get an edge over their rivals by introducing strong security measures, allowing them to attract and maintain clients who value security and privacy.

3. **Compliance:** To secure sensitive data, several regulatory authorities demand that corporations put strong security measures in place. Threat modeling can assist businesses in proving that they adhere to compliance standards.

4. **Reduced Legal Liability:** Data breaches and other security incidents can result in significant legal liability for businesses. By implementing appropriate security measures, businesses can reduce the risk of legal liability and protect themselves from potential lawsuits.

5. **Cost Savings:** Threat modeling can help businesses identify potential security risks early in the development process, reducing the cost of implementing security measures. This can result in significant cost savings over time.

In conclusion, threat modeling provides numerous technical and business benefits. Businesses can protect their valuable assets, reputation, and customer trust by identifying potential security risks early in development and implementing appropriate security measures. Threat modeling can also help businesses gain a competitive advantage, meet regulatory requirements, and reduce the cost of implementing security measures.

Threat Modeling Processes

Threat modeling is a systematic process that identifies and addresses potential security risks in software systems or applications. The threat modeling method involves several steps that enable developers to remember potential security risks and manage them systematically. Some of the various processes involved in threat modeling are:

1. Identify the System or Application to be Modeled

Identifying the system or application to be modeled is the initial step in the threat modeling process. Understanding the function, architecture, and parts of the system or software is necessary for this. This step aims to establish a clear understanding of the system or application being modeled so that potential security risks can be identified and addressed.

2. Identify and Document the Assets

The assets the system or application intends to protect are identified and documented in the following step in the threat modeling process. These assets may include data, hardware, software, intellectual property, and other resources that are critical to the operation of the system or application. This step aims to establish a clear understanding of the assets that are being protected so that potential security risks can be identified and addressed.

3. Create a Data Flow Diagram

A data flow diagram (DFD) is used to visualize the data flow through the system or application. This helps identify potential security risks and enables developers to design appropriate security controls to mitigate those risks. The DFD determines the various inputs, processes, and outputs of the system or application and the multiple actors and components involved in the system or application.

4. Identify Threats and Attack Vectors

Threats are potential risks to the system or application's security, while attack vectors are the methods attackers may use to exploit those threats. Identifying threats and attack vectors enables developers to understand the potential risks to the system or application and to design appropriate security controls. This step aims to identify the various threats and attack vectors that could be used to compromise the system or application.

5. Evaluate Risks

The next step is to evaluate the risks associated with each threat and attack vector. This process analyzes each threat's likelihood and potential impact as well as the level of risk it poses. This step aims to evaluate the potential impact of each threat and attack vector and prioritize the risks based on their potential impact.

6. Design and Implement Security Controls

Based on the risks identified in the previous step, developers design and implement appropriate security controls to mitigate those risks. These controls may include access controls, encryption, intrusion detection systems, and other measures to protect the system or application from potential threats. This step aims to design and implement adequate security controls that address the potential security risks identified in the previous actions.

7. Test and Validate the Model

Once the security controls have been designed and implemented, the model is tested and validated to ensure it mitigates potential security risks effectively. This involves simulating possible attacks and assessing the effectiveness of the security controls in preventing or mitigating those attacks. This step aims to validate the effectiveness of the security controls and identify any potential weaknesses or vulnerabilities that need to be addressed.

8. Review and Update the Model

Finally, the threat model is reviewed and updated regularly to ensure that it effectively addresses potential security risks. This involves assessing new threats and attack vectors and updating the security controls to ensure they mitigate those risks effectively. This step ensures that the threat model effectively addresses potential security risks over time.

Threat Modeling Techniques

Threat modeling is essential to modern security practices, enabling developers to proactively identify and mitigate potential security threats before attackers can exploit them. It is a collaborative exercise involving multiple stakeholders and should be conducted throughout the development lifecycle to identify and address new and emerging threats. By incorporating threat modeling into their security practices, organizations can ensure that their systems and applications remain secure in the face of new and emerging threats. The threat modeling techniques include:

Data Flow Diagram (DFD) threat modeling

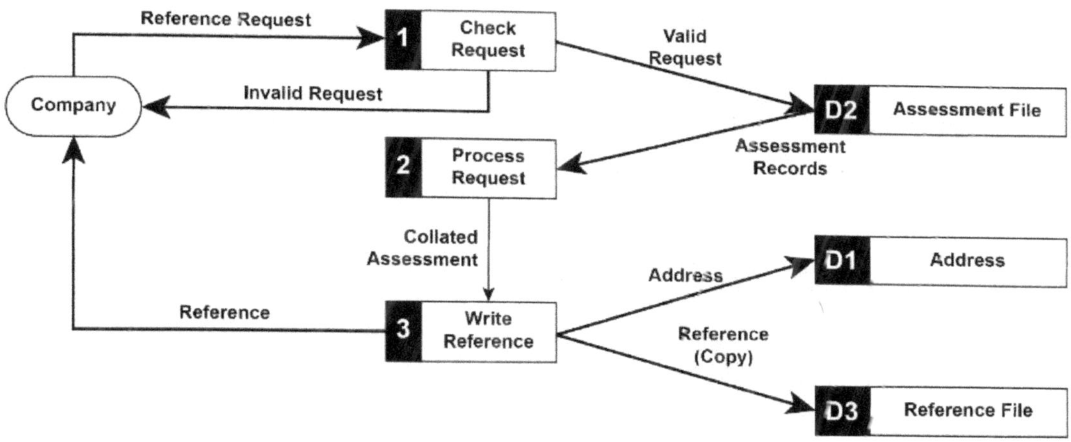

This technique is widely used for identifying an application's potential security risks and vulnerabilities. This technique involves visualizing an application's data flow and analyzing it for potential security risks, such as unauthorized data access, data breaches, or data loss.

The first step in DFD threat modeling is to create a data flow diagram of the application. This diagram should include all inputs, outputs, and data flow within the application and any external systems or data sources that interact with the application. The chart should be as detailed as possible to ensure that all potential security risks are identified.

Once the data flow diagram has been created, the next step is to analyze it for potential security risks. This involves identifying all potential threats to the application's data flow, such as unauthorized access, modification, or data destruction. It is also important to consider potential threats from external sources, such as hackers or malware.

Evaluating each threat's likelihood and potential impact comes next after potential threats have been identified. This involves considering factors such as the sensitivity of the data, the ease of exploitation, and the potential impact on the organization if the threat is realized. This information can then be used to prioritize security risks and develop appropriate mitigation strategies.

Benefits of the DFD

1. **Provides a visual representation of the system:** DFD threat modeling offers a visual representation of the flow of data through a system, which can help teams better understand the system's architecture and identify potential vulnerabilities.

2. **Easy to understand:** DFD threat modeling is easy to understand and can be used by technical and non-technical team members. This makes it a valuable tool for teams with varying levels of expertise.

3. **Can be used to model complex systems:** DFD threat modeling can be used to model complex systems with multiple data flows, making it a flexible approach that can be adapted to a wide range of techniques.

4. **Supports risk analysis:** DFD threat modeling can perform risk analysis by identifying potential threats and vulnerabilities and assigning a risk level. This can help teams prioritize their efforts and address the most critical threats.

DFD Threat Modeling Drawbacks

1. **Limited scope:** Since DFD threat modeling focuses on the data flow through a system rather than all possible system risks, specific threats may need to be addressed.

2. **Can be time-consuming:** DFD threat modeling can be a time-consuming process, particularly for large and complex systems, and this may require a significant investment of time and resources.

3. **May require technical expertise:** While DFD threat modeling is generally easy to understand, it may require some technical expertise to leverage its benefits fully. Teams with limited technical expertise may need help to implement this approach effectively.

4. **May require frequent updates:** DFD threat modeling may require frequent updates as the system evolves, and this can be a challenge for teams working on rapidly changing systems.

Overall, DFD threat modeling is a valuable approach to threat modeling that can help teams identify potential threats and vulnerabilities in a system. However, it should be used with other methodologies and tailored to the team's needs and the system being analyzed.

Attack Tree modeling

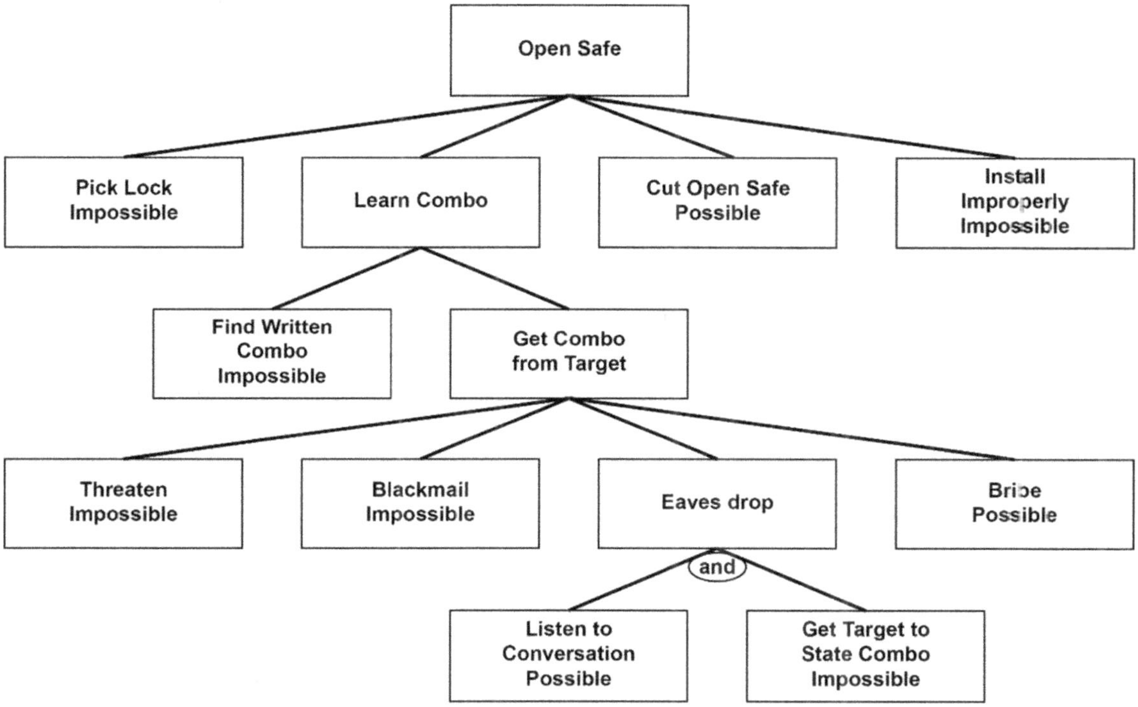

Attack Tree modeling is a widely used technique in information security for identifying and analyzing potential attack scenarios on an information system. It is a visual tool used to illustrate the structure of attack scenarios and to explore the potential weaknesses in a system that could lead to such an attack.

The basis of the Attack Tree modeling technique is a tree-like structure that starts with the attack goal or objective at the top of the tree and branches out into sub-trees representing the different ways the plan can be achieved. Each sub-tree represents a different attack scenario, with each branch representing an extra step in the attack process. The tree leaves represent the specific actions an attacker could take to achieve their goal.

The Attack Tree modeling technique analyzes the tree's different branches and leaves to identify the system's weakest points and develop effective mitigation strategies. This is done by identifying the specific conditions that must be met to achieve their goal and then analyzing the different steps and actions an attacker could take to exploit those conditions.

Benefits Of Attack Tree Modeling

1. **Systematic approach:** Attack tree modeling provides a systematic approach to assessing security risks and identifying potential vulnerabilities in a system.

2. **Effective risk management:** Organizations can focus their resources and efforts on mitigating the most critical risks by identifying and prioritizing the most likely attack scenarios.

3. **Better decision-making:** Attack tree modeling gives decision-makers a comprehensive grasp of the risks associated with distinct attack scenarios, enabling them to choose measures to mitigate risks with knowledge.

4. **Cost-effective:** Attack tree modeling is a cost-effective way to assess security risks, as it can be performed relatively quickly and does not require a large team of experts.

Drawbacks of Attack Tree Modeling

1. **Complexity**: Attack tree modeling can be complex, particularly when dealing with large or complex systems. This complexity can make it challenging to identify all potential attack scenarios and prioritize them effectively.
2. **Limited scope:** Attack tree modeling only focuses on external threats and does not consider internal threats or vulnerabilities that may arise from within the organization.
3. **Limited accuracy:** Attack tree modeling relies on assumptions and estimates about the likelihood and impact of various attack scenarios, which may only sometimes be accurate or up to date.
4. **Time-consuming:** Attack tree modeling can be time-consuming, mainly when dealing with complex systems or large organizations. This can make it challenging to keep the attack tree model up-to-date and relevant over time.

In conclusion, Attack Tree modeling is a powerful tool for analyzing potential attack scenarios and identifying vulnerabilities in an information system. By using this technique, organizations can better understand their risks and develop effective mitigation strategies. Attack Tree modeling should be considered an essential component of any comprehensive information security program.

PASTA Threat Modeling

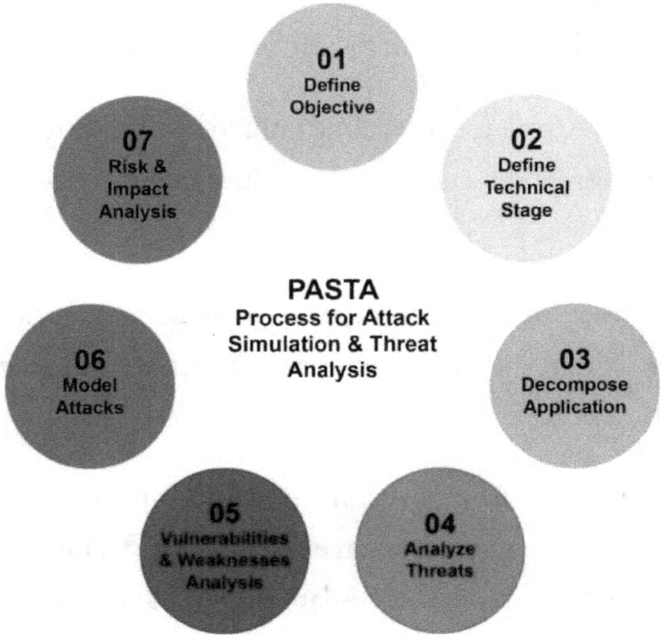

PASTA (Process for Attack Simulation and Threat Analysis) is a threat modeling methodology widely used in information security. This methodology is based on simulating real-world attack scenarios to identify potential vulnerabilities in an information system.

The seven phase PASTA Methodology:

1. **Preparation:** In this phase, the scope of the threat modeling exercise is defined, and the objectives of the practice are established. The team responsible for the training is also assembled during this phase.

2. **Asset profiling:** This phase involves identifying and categorizing the assets that are being protected by the information system. This includes data, hardware, software, and other components.

3. **Threat modeling:** In this phase, potential threats to the system are identified and analyzed. This includes identifying the threat agents, such as hackers or malware, and the attack vectors that they could use to exploit vulnerabilities in the system.

4. **Vulnerability analysis:** This phase involves identifying potential vulnerabilities in the system that attackers could exploit. This includes analyzing the different layers of the system, such as the network, applications, and operating systems, to identify potential weaknesses.

5. **Risk assessment:** In this phase, the risks associated with each potential vulnerability are assessed, including the likelihood of an attack occurring and the potential impact of a successful attack.

6. **Mitigation planning:** Based on the risk assessment results, mitigation strategies are developed to address the identified vulnerabilities and reduce the overall risk to the system.

7. **Reporting:** In this final phase, the results of the threat modeling exercise are documented and communicated to stakeholders, including technical teams, management, and business leaders.

This includes providing recommendations for mitigation strategies and highlighting areas of ongoing risk.

Benefits of PASTA Threat Modeling

1. **Comprehensive analysis:** PASTA provides a comprehensive analysis of security threats, vulnerabilities, and risks, allowing organizations to prioritize and address the most critical issues.
2. **Customizable approach:** PASTA is highly customizable and can be adapted to fit an organization's specific needs, making it an effective tool for various industries and systems.
3. **Collaborative process:** PASTA involves stakeholders from across an organization, including IT, security, and business teams, to ensure that all perspectives are considered and that the resulting analysis is well-rounded.
4. **Repeatable process:** PASTA is a repeatable process, allowing organizations to continuously assess and improve their security posture over time.

Drawbacks of PASTA Threat Modeling

1. **Resource-intensive:** PASTA can be a resource-intensive process, requiring a significant investment of time and expertise to conduct a thorough analysis.
2. **Complexity**: PASTA can be complex, particularly for organizations with large or complex systems, and may require significant effort to ensure that all potential threats and vulnerabilities are identified.
3. **Limited accuracy:** PASTA, like any threat modeling methodology, relies on assumptions and estimates, which may only sometimes be accurate or up-to-date.

4. **Requires expertise:** PASTA requires expertise in threat modeling and the specific systems and technologies being analyzed, making it easier for organizations with a dedicated security team or access to external experts

PASTA is a powerful threat modeling methodology widely used in information security. Organizations can comprehensively understand their risks and develop effective mitigation strategies by simulating real-world attack scenarios and analyzing potential vulnerabilities. PASTA should be considered an essential component of any comprehensive information security program.

STRIDE Threat Modeling

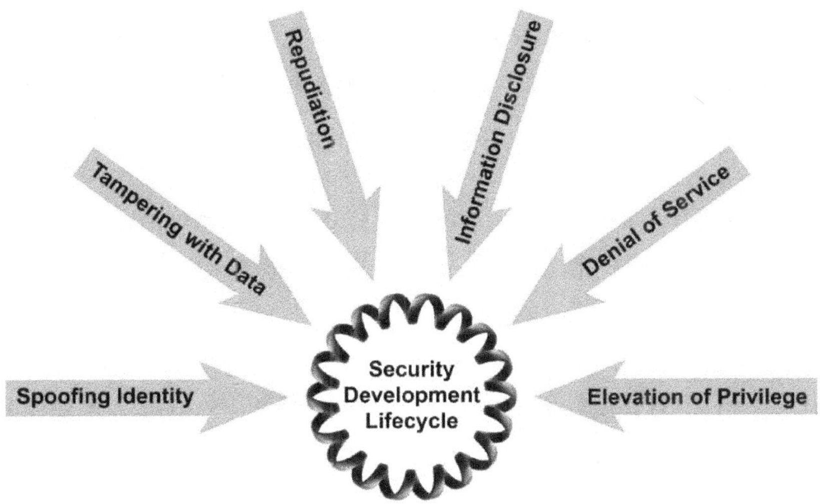

STRIDE is a threat modeling methodology widely used in the field of information security. This methodology provides a framework for identifying and addressing potential threats to information systems based on six different categories: spoofing, tampering, repudiating, disclosing information, denying service, and elevating privilege.

1. **Spoofing** refers to an attacker pretending to be someone else, such as a legitimate user or system. This can include attacks such as phishing or using forged digital certificates.

2. **Tampering** involves the modification of data or systems by an attacker. This can include attacks such as SQL injection or configuring configuration files.

3. **Repudiation** refers to an attacker's ability to deny taking a particular action. This can include attacks such as the manipulation of audit logs or the use of anonymous communication channels.

4. **Information Disclosure** involves the unauthorized access to or disclosure of sensitive information. This can include attacks such as the theft of passwords or the use of insecure communication channels.

5. **Denial of Service** involves an attacker's ability to prevent legitimate users from accessing the system. This can include distributed denial of service (DDoS) attacks or resource exhaustion attacks.

6. **Elevation of Privilege** involves an attacker's ability to access system resources or data they are not authorized to access. This can include attacks such as privilege escalation or exploiting vulnerabilities in access controls.

Benefits of STRIDE

Structured approach: The STRIDE approach provides a structured methodology for identifying potential threats based on six categories of attacks: spoofing, tampering, repudiation, information disclosure, denial of service, and elevation of privilege. This structured approach makes it easier for teams to identify potential threats and develop appropriate security controls and measures.

1. **Comprehensive coverage:** The six categories of attacks covered by STRIDE provide comprehensive coverage of potential threats to a system. This ensures that teams can identify and address various potential threats.

2. **Easy to understand**: The STRIDE approach is easy to understand and can be applied by both technical and non-technical team members. This makes it a valuable tool for teams with varying levels of expertise.

3. **Integration with other methodologies:** The STRIDE approach can be easily integrated with different methods, such as threat modeling using attack trees or PASTA. This flexibility allows teams to tailor their threat modeling approach to their needs.

Drawbacks of STRIDE

1. **Limited scope:** The STRIDE approach focuses on six categories of attacks and may not identify all potential threats to a system. This may result in some threats needing to be addressed.

2. **Lack of granularity**: The STRIDE approach needs to provide a granular level of detail about potential threats. This may make it difficult for teams to develop appropriate security controls and measures.

3. **Over-reliance on technical expertise:** The STRIDE approach may be more effective when used by teams with high technical knowledge. Teams with limited technical expertise may only be able to leverage this approach's benefits partially.

4. **Potential for false positives:** The STRIDE approach may identify threats irrelevant to the analyzed system. This can result in false positives that may divert resources from addressing more critical threats.

Overall, the STRIDE approach is a valuable tool for identifying potential threats to a system. However, it should be used with other methodologies and tailored to the team's needs and the system being analyzed.

Trike threat modeling

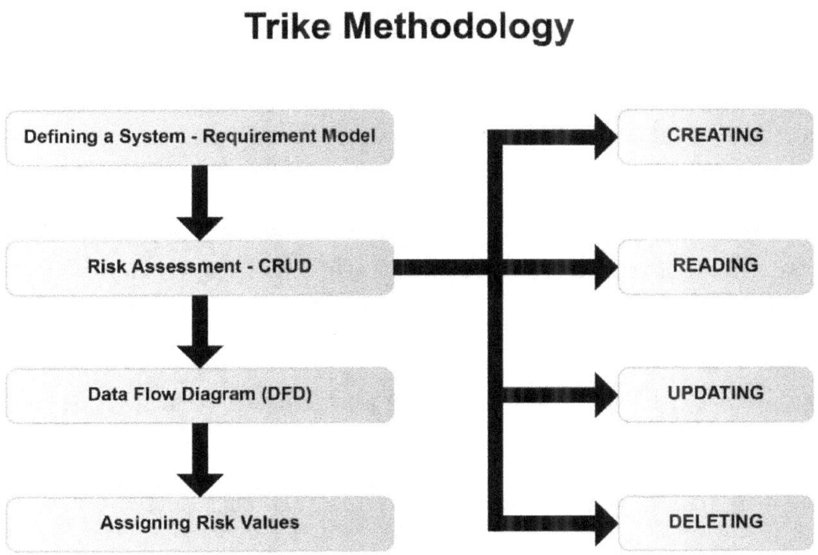

Trike threat modeling is a relatively new methodology for identifying and addressing threats to information systems. This methodology is based on "threat refinement," which involves breaking down high-level threats into smaller, more manageable components.

The Trike methodology is designed to be flexible and adaptable, allowing organizations to customize the methods to their specific needs and requirements. This involves defining the scope of the analysis, selecting the appropriate threat modeling techniques, and identifying the relevant assets and stakeholders.

The Trike methodology in four steps:

1. **Decomposition:** This involves breaking down the system into smaller components, such as data flows, processes, and assets.

2. **Threat identification:** This involves identifying potential threats to each component based on known attack vectors and threat scenarios.

3. **Attack simulation:** This involves simulating potential attacks against the system, using various techniques such as penetration testing, vulnerability scanning, and social engineering.

4. **Mitigation:** This involves developing and implementing strategies to mitigate identified threats, such as implementing additional security controls or modifying existing controls to address identified vulnerabilities better.

Benefits of Trike

1. **Customizable approach:** Trike is highly customizable and can be adapted to fit an organization's specific needs, making it an effective tool for various industries and systems.

2. **Simplified process:** Trike provides a streamlined process for identifying and analyzing security threats, making it easier for organizations with limited security expertise to conduct a thorough analysis.

3. **Collaborative process:** Trike involves stakeholders from across an organization, including IT, security, and business teams, to ensure that all perspectives are considered and that the resulting analysis is well-rounded.

4. **Repeatable process:** Trike is a repeatable process, allowing organizations to continuously assess and improve their security posture.

Drawbacks of Trike Threat Modeling

1. **Limited scope:** Trike focuses primarily on external threats and does not consider internal threats or vulnerabilities that may arise from within the organization.

2. **Limited accuracy:** Trike, like any threat modeling methodology, relies on assumptions and estimates, which may only sometimes be accurate or up to date.

3. **Less comprehensive:** Trike may be less comprehensive than other threat modeling methodologies, particularly for organizations with large or complex systems.

4. **Requires expertise:** Trike requires expertise in threat modeling and the specific systems and technologies being analyzed, making it easier for organizations with a dedicated security team or access to external experts.

Overall, the Trike threat modeling methodology provides a structured and adaptable approach to identifying and addressing potential threats to information systems. Organizations can better understand their risks and develop effective mitigation strategies by breaking down threats into smaller components and focusing on simulation and testing.

VAST

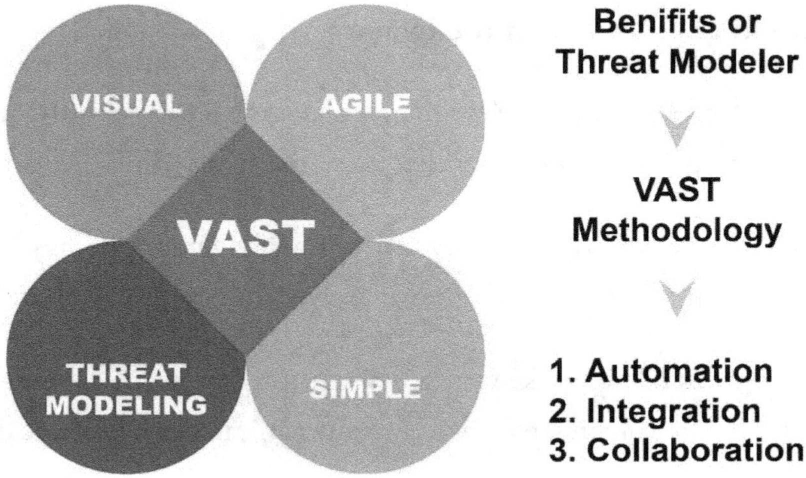

VAST stands for Visual, Agile, and Simple Threat modeling, and it is a methodology for threat modeling that focuses on being lightweight and easy to use. VAST aims to provide a simple and effective way for organizations to identify and address security threats.

Benefits of VAST

1. **Lightweight:** VAST is a lightweight methodology that is easy to learn and implement, making it accessible to organizations with limited security expertise.

2. **Agile:** VAST is designed to be an agile methodology, allowing organizations to quickly adapt to changes in their environment and address new security threats as they emerge.

3. **Visual:** VAST uses visual representations to help stakeholders understand the security threats and vulnerabilities associated with their systems, making it easier to communicate and collaborate.

4. **Simple:** VAST is a simple methodology that focuses on the most critical security threats, making it easier for organizations to prioritize and address their most significant risks.

Drawbacks of VAST

1. **Limited scope:** VAST may be less comprehensive than other threat modeling methodologies, particularly for organizations with large or complex systems.

2. **Limited accuracy:** VAST, like any threat modeling methodology, relies on assumptions and estimates, which may only sometimes be accurate or up to date.

3. **Less collaborative:** VAST may be less coordinated than other methodologies, as it focuses primarily on the expertise of a single individual or team rather than involving stakeholders from across the organization.

4. **Less customizable:** VAST may be less customizable than other methodologies, as it focuses on specific techniques and practices. Organizations may need help adapting VAST to fit their needs or requirements.

CAPEC

CAPEC stands for Common Attack Pattern Enumeration and Classification: This is a comprehensive list of known attack patterns that can be used to identify potential threats and vulnerabilities in a system or application. The CAPEC list includes a detailed description of each attack pattern, the typical sequence of events involved, and the possible consequences or impacts.

CAPEC was created by MITRE Corporation, a non-profit organization that operates federally funded research and development centers, and a community of security experts maintains it. The purpose of CAPEC is to provide a standardized way of describing and categorizing attack patterns, which can be used by security analysts, software developers, and other stakeholders to understand and mitigate potential security risks.

Benefits of CAPEC

1. **Standardization:** CAPEC provides a standardized way of describing and categorizing attack patterns, making it easier for security analysts and developers to understand and mitigate potential security risks.

2. **Comprehensive:** The CAPEC list is extensive, covering a wide range of known attack patterns, which can help organizations identify potential attack vectors and prioritize their security efforts.

3. **Up to date:** The CAPEC list is updated regularly to reflect emerging threats, ensuring organizations can access the latest information on potential security risks.

4. **Community-driven:** CAPEC is maintained by a community of security experts, which helps ensure that it is a reliable and well-vetted resource.

Drawbacks of CAPEC

1. **Complexity:** The CAPEC list can be extensive and complex, making it challenging for some organizations to use and apply it effectively.

2. **Limited scope**: CAPEC primarily focuses on known attack patterns, which means it may only sometimes be effective in identifying new or emerging threats.

3. **False positives:** Some attack patterns listed in CAPEC may not be relevant to a particular organization or application, which can lead to false positives and unnecessary security efforts.

4. **Overreliance:** Organizations may become over-reliant on CAPEC and fail to adequately assess and address unique security risks and vulnerabilities specific to their applications or systems.

While CAPEC can be a valuable resource for organizations seeking to identify and mitigate potential security risks, it is essential to use it as part of a broader, risk-based approach to security rather than relying solely on its categorization of known attack patterns.

In conclusion, several threat modeling techniques can be used to assess security risks in applications. Each method can be used to find a particular risk and has benefits and drawbacks. By combining these techniques, organizations can develop a comprehensive threat model that provides a detailed understanding of potential security risks and vulnerabilities in their applications.

Integrating Threat Modeling into the SDLC

Integrating threat modeling into the software development life cycle (SDLC) refers to proactively identifying and mitigating potential security risks at every stage of software development. It involves using a systematic approach to identify the potential threats to a system, evaluate their likelihood and potential impact, and then develop and implement appropriate countermeasures to prevent or mitigate those threats.

Threat modeling can be integrated into the SDLC in various ways, such as incorporating it into the planning, design, development, testing, and maintenance phases. By doing so, developers can identify and address potential security weaknesses early in the development process, reducing the likelihood of security breaches and minimizing the potential impact of any security incidents.

Integrating threat modeling into the SDLC is essential to building secure and resilient software systems. Developers might leverage technology that is more resilient to cyberattacks, protect sensitive data, and uphold the trust of users and stakeholders by being proactive in recognizing and mitigating potential security threats.

Incorporating Threat Modeling in The Planning Phase

In the planning phase, incorporating threat modeling refers to proactively identifying and mitigating potential security risks at the earliest stage of software development. It involves incorporating threat modeling techniques into the software development life cycle (SDLC) planning phase to identify potential security risks and develop appropriate countermeasures.

Incorporating threat modeling in the planning phase entails several vital steps to identify and mitigate potential security risks in software development. These steps include:

1. **Identify Assets and Data:** The first step is identifying the assets and data that need protection. This includes identifying sensitive data, system components, and infrastructure critical to the software system's functioning.

2. **Analyze Threats and Vulnerabilities:** After identifying assets and data, the following stage examines potential risks and vulnerabilities that could threaten the system's security. This entails thinking through numerous scenarios in which an attacker could take advantage of a vulnerability and harm the system.

3. **Develop Countermeasures:** Based on the identified threats and vulnerabilities, developers can develop and implement appropriate countermeasures to prevent or mitigate those threats. This may involve implementing secure coding practices, access controls, encryption, and other security measures.

4. **Prioritize Risks:** Because not all risks are created equal, developers must rank them according to how likely they are and how they might affect the system. Prioritizing the most serious threats helps guarantee that resources are deployed efficiently.

5. **Review and Refine:** Finally, reviewing and refining the threat model regularly throughout the planning phase is critical to ensure that it remains up-to-date and effective. This involves re-evaluating the identified risks and countermeasures and making adjustments as necessary.

Incorporating Threat Modeling in the Planning Phase

1. **Early Identification of Risks:** Incorporating threat modeling in the planning phase allows developers to identify potential security risks early in the software development life cycle. By doing so, developers can address these risks proactively, reducing the likelihood of security breaches and minimizing the potential impact of any security incidents.

2. **Better Resource Allocation:** Incorporating threat modeling in the planning phase allows developers to allocate resources effectively. By identifying potential risks early, developers can prioritize the implementation of countermeasures, reducing the risk of resource wastage and ensuring that the most critical threats are addressed first.

3. **Improved Collaboration:** Incorporating threat modeling in the planning phase facilitates collaboration between various stakeholders in the software development process. This includes developers, security professionals, project managers, and other relevant parties. By involving these stakeholders in the threat modeling process, developers can ensure that all parties understand the risks and potential consequences of potential security incidents and work together to develop effective countermeasures.

Challenges of Incorporating Threat Modeling in the Planning Phase

1. **Lack of Expertise:** Incorporating threat modeling in the planning phase requires expertise in the field of security. Many developers may need this expertise, making identifying potential security risks and developing appropriate countermeasures difficult.

2. **Time Constraints:** Incorporating threat modeling in the planning phase may add time to the software development process. This may be challenging, especially in projects with tight deadlines or limited resources.

3. **Difficulty in Quantifying Risks:** More than identifying potential security risks is needed, and developers need to quantify these risks to determine their potential impact and develop appropriate countermeasures. However, quantifying risks can be challenging, especially when dealing with new or unknown threats.

Implementing Threat Modeling During Design and Development

Implementing threat modeling during design and development involves analyzing the system and its components to identify potential threats, assessing the likelihood and impact of those threats, and then implementing appropriate controls to mitigate or eliminate those threats.

1. Identify the assets and threats

The first step in implementing threat modeling during design and development is to identify the assets that need to be protected and the potential threats that could compromise those assets. Support can include data, software, hardware, and people, and threats can come from internal or external sources, such as hackers, viruses, or employee errors.

2. **Create a data flow diagram**

   A data flow diagram (DFD) visually represents data flow through a system. Creating a DFD can help identify potential threats to the system, and it can also help identify where security controls are necessary. The DFD can map out how data flows through the system, including how it's collected, stored, and transmitted.

3. **Identify the entry and exit points**

   Once the DFD is created, it's essential to identify the entry and exit points. Entry points are places where data enters the system, such as through a user interface or network connection. Exit points are where data leaves the system, such as through a report or network transmission.

4. **Identify the vulnerabilities**

   After identifying the entry and exit points, it's essential to identify potential vulnerabilities that exist at these points. Vulnerabilities can be in the software, hardware, or processes used to handle data. For example, an exposure could be a lack of encryption when transmitting sensitive data.

5. **Prioritize the threats**

   Once the vulnerabilities are identified, it's essential to prioritize the threats based on their potential impact on the system. Threats that could cause the most damage should be given the highest priority.

6. Develop mitigation strategies

After prioritizing the threats, the next step is to develop mitigation strategies to address them. Mitigation strategies include adding security controls, implementing encryption, or changing the software design to eliminate vulnerabilities.

7. Continuously monitor and update

Finally, it's essential to continuously monitor the system and update the threat model as needed. As new threats are identified or the system changes, the threat model should be updated to reflect those changes.

Implementing threat modeling during design and development can help identify potential security risks early in development. By identifying and addressing these risks, developers can ensure that the final product is secure and minimize the risk of security vulnerabilities.

Threat Modeling Early

1. **Early detection of security vulnerabilities:** By implementing threat modeling during the design and development phase, security vulnerabilities can be identified and addressed before the system is deployed, reducing the risk of security breaches.

2. **Reduced cost of remediation:** Identifying and addressing security vulnerabilities early in the development process diminishes the cost of remediation because security issues after deploying the system can be significantly more expensive.

3. **Improved security posture:** Implementing threat modeling during design and development helps to create a more secure system, reducing the risk of data breaches, financial losses, and reputational damage.

4. **Better alignment with regulatory requirements:** Many regulations and standards require threat modeling in the software development process. Implementing threat modeling helps ensure compliance with these requirements.

Threat Modeling later in the SDLC

1. **Time-consuming:** Implementing threat modeling can be time-consuming, particularly for complex systems. This can lead to delays in the development process, which can be a disadvantage for organizations that need to deliver products quickly.

2. **Resource-intensive:** Threat modeling requires security and risk management expertise, which may be difficult for organizations to find and retain. This can lead to higher costs for organizations that need to hire or train security professionals.

3. **False sense of security:** Threat modeling can give organizations a false sense of security if it is not done thoroughly. This can lead to vulnerabilities being missed, which attackers can exploit.

4. **Limited effectiveness:** Threat modeling is not a silver bullet for security; it is just one tool in a more extensive security program. There may be a need for more than threat modeling to secure a system. Organizations must also implement other security measures, such as vulnerability assessments, penetration testing, and secure coding practices, to create a more secure system.

Continuous Threat Modeling

Continuous Threat Modeling during maintenance is the ongoing process of identifying, assessing, and prioritizing potential security threats and vulnerabilities to an application or system during maintenance. It involves continuously monitoring the system for changes that may introduce new security risks, such as updates to third-party libraries or changes in software or hardware. Organizations can implement effective security measures and reduce the likelihood of costly security breaches or attacks by continually assessing and analyzing the system for potential vulnerabilities and threats.

Best Practices for Continuous Threat Modeling During Maintenance

1. **Define a process:** Organizations should define a process for continuous threat modeling during maintenance that includes the steps, the tools to be used, and the roles and responsibilities of the various stakeholders involved.

2. **Prioritize threats:** It is essential to prioritize threats based on their severity and impact on the system, and this will help organizations focus on addressing the most critical vulnerabilities first.

3. **Involve all stakeholders:** All stakeholders, including developers, security teams, and business analysts, should be involved in the continuous threat modeling process. This will ensure that all potential threats are identified and addressed.

4. **Use automated tools:** Automated tools such as static code analyzers and vulnerability scanners can help identify potential vulnerabilities and threats more efficiently than manual processes.

5. **Monitor and update:** Organizations should continuously monitor and update their threat modeling process to ensure that it remains practical and relevant as the system evolves.

Benefits of Continuous Threat Modeling During Maintenance

1. **Early Detection of Vulnerabilities:** Continuous threat modeling during maintenance helps to identify vulnerabilities and potential threats before they can be exploited. This reduces the likelihood of a security breach and helps to keep systems secure.

2. **Reduced Costs:** Addressing vulnerabilities and threats during maintenance is typically less expensive than dealing with a security breach or attack after deployment. Continuous threat modeling helps organizations identify and address vulnerabilities early on, reducing the likelihood of costly incidents.

3. **Improved Compliance:** Continuous threat modeling helps organizations stay compliant with industry regulations and standards by ensuring that security is a priority throughout the entire software development lifecycle.

4. **Greater Visibility:** Continuous threat modeling provides greater visibility into the system, enabling organizations to identify potential vulnerabilities and threats that may have been missed during the initial design and development phase.

5. **Better Communication:** By involving all stakeholders in the continuous threat modeling process, organizations can improve team communication and collaboration, leading to more effective security measures.

Continuous Threat Modeling During Maintenance Challenges

1. **Increased Time and Resource Requirements:** Continuous threat modeling during maintenance requires ongoing resources and can be time-consuming. This can challenge organizations that need more resources to devote to this process.

2. **False Positives:** Automated tools used in continuous threat modeling can generate false positives, wasting resources and unnecessary efforts to address non-existent vulnerabilities.

3. **Lack of Awareness:** Stakeholders may need to be made aware of the importance of continuous threat modeling or may need to have the necessary expertise to participate effectively in the process. This can lead to a lack of engagement or ineffective efforts to address vulnerabilities.

4. **Over-Reliance on Automated Tools:** While automated tools can help identify vulnerabilities and threats, organizations should rely on more than these tools. Manual review and analysis are still necessary to identify and address all potential vulnerabilities.

5. **Resistance to Change:** Organizations not used to continuous threat modeling may resist change and may be reluctant to allocate resources or change established processes.

Continuous threat modeling during maintenance is a critical process that helps ensure an application's security even after it has been deployed. By continuously identifying and assessing potential threats, vulnerabilities, and risks, organizations can proactively mitigate security issues before they become serious problems. This approach requires ongoing collaboration between developers, security teams, and other stakeholders to stay on top of emerging threats and promptly adjust security measures. This is an essential practice for any organization that takes the security of its applications and systems seriously.

Organizations can save time, reduce costs, and improve their overall security posture by identifying potential security threats early in development. While implementing threat modeling may require additional time, resources, and expertise, the benefits far outweigh the potential drawbacks.

The advantages of early risk identification, efficient resource allocation, and improved teamwork make this strategy beneficial despite certain difficulties. All firms that produce software ought to prioritize it since doing so can make the internet safer and more secure for everyone. With the growing threat landscape and the increasing sophistication of attackers, organizations must prioritize security in their software development processes. By doing so, developers can ensure that their software systems are secure, resilient, and meet the expectations of their users and stakeholders.

Application Programming Interfaces (APIs)

What is an API?

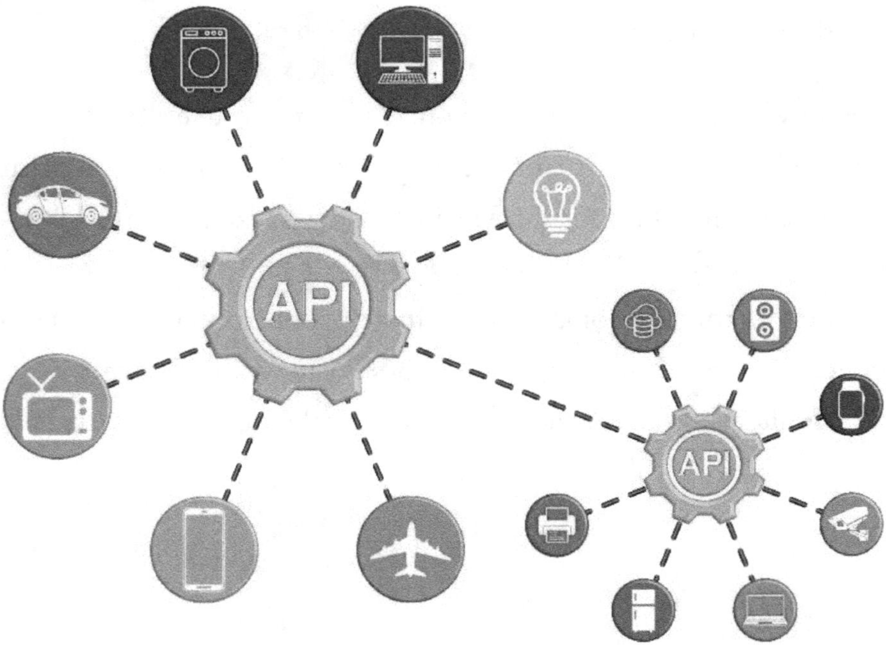

An Application Programming Interface (API) is a set of protocols, tools, and methods that enable different software applications to communicate and interact. An API defines the rules and specifications for how other applications can request or exchange data, services, or functionality from one another.

An API acts as an intermediary between two or more applications, allowing them to communicate and interact seamlessly. The API typically provides a standardized interface that enables one application to access the services or data of another application without needing to know the underlying implementation details or programming language.

APIs can be classified into different categories depending on their level of abstraction and the types of services they provide. Some common types of APIs include web APIs, which allow web applications to access data or functionality from web services; operating system APIs, which provide low-level access to system resources and hardware devices; and programming language APIs, which define the syntax and semantics of programming languages and provide libraries of pre-built functions and data structures.

APIs have become increasingly important in modern software development, as they enable developers to build more complex and integrated applications by leveraging the capabilities of other services and systems. APIs are used extensively in web and mobile app development, cloud computing, and the Internet of Things (IoT), among other areas.

How APIs work

APIs work by following a set of protocols and standards that enable different applications to communicate with each other. Here is a high-level overview of how APIs work:

6. **Request:** The first step in the API process is to send a request from the client application to the API. The proposal includes the following:

- ➢ the desired data or functionality
- ➢ the request method (GET, POST, PUT, DELETE, etc.)

- any required parameters or data

7. **Processing:** Once the API receives the request, it processes it by validating the request parameters, performing required actions, and retrieving or updating data, as necessary.

8. **Response:** After processing the request, the API responds to the client application. The response includes any requested data or functionality and relevant metadata or status codes. The answer is typically sent in a standardized format such as JSON, XML, or HTML.

9. **Error Handling:** If an error occurs during any step of the API process, the API sends an error response back to the client application. The error response includes a status code and a description of the error.

API follows specific architectural patterns and standards, enabling application interoperability and compatibility. The most common architectural API designs are REST (Representational State Transfer) and SOAP (Simple Object Access Protocol).

Types of Web APIs

1. Representational State Transfer (REST) APIs

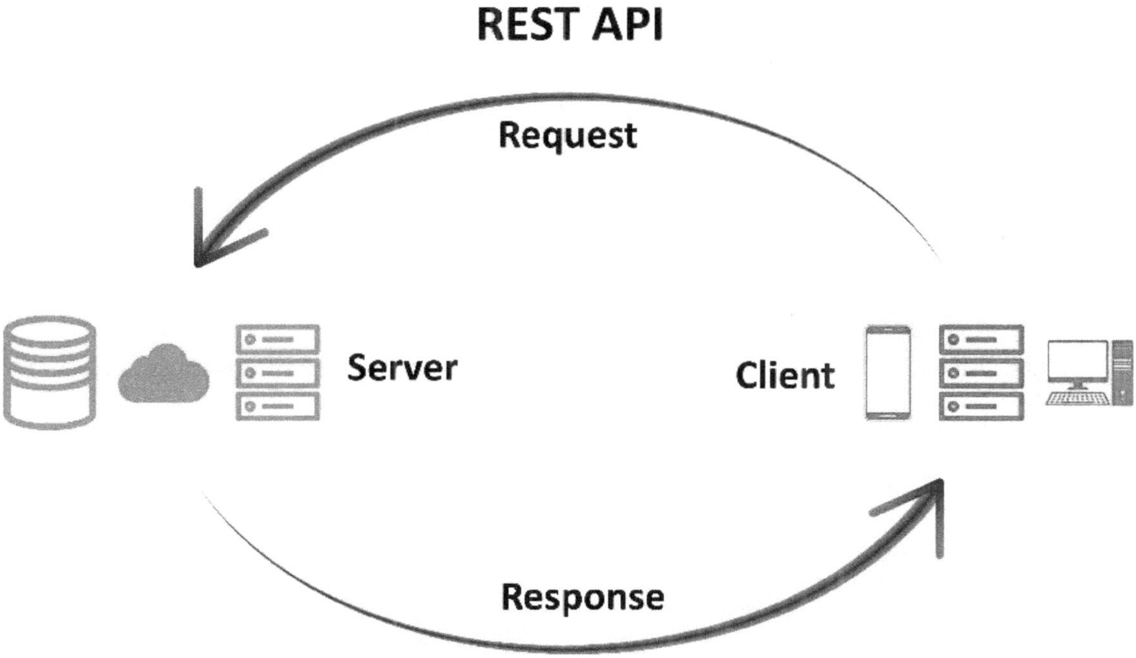

Representational State Transfer (REST) APIs are a widely used type of web API that enables the exchange of data and resources between different systems and applications. REST APIs are used in various applications and systems, including web and mobile applications, Internet of Things (IoT) devices, and cloud services. They use HTTP requests to retrieve or modify data and are designed to be simple, scalable, and flexible.

REST APIs are based on a few fundamental principles that define how they should function and be used. These principles include:

- **Resource Identification:** REST APIs are based on the idea of resources, which are identified by a unique URL or Uniform Resource Identifier (URI). Each resource represents a specific object or piece of data that can be accessed, modified, or deleted using HTTP requests.

- **Uniform Interface:** REST APIs use a consistent interface for accessing and manipulating resources, which includes four main methods or operations: GET, POST, PUT, and DELETE. Each method has a specific purpose and behavior, enabling various resource interactions.

- **Stateless Interaction:** REST APIs are stateless, which means that each request to the API contains all the information needed to complete the request. This enables greater scalability and flexibility, as recommendations can be handled independently without reliance on previous requests or states.

- **Client-Server Architecture:** REST APIs use a client-server architecture, which separates the concerns of the client and server and enables greater modularity and flexibility.

- **Cache-ability:** REST APIs support caching, improving performance, and reducing the server load by allowing clients to store and reuse responses from previous requests.

To use a REST API, a client application sends HTTP requests to the API, which returns a response in a specific format, such as XML or JSON. The client can then parse and use the response data as needed. REST APIs are often preferred over other APIs for their simplicity, scalability, and flexibility and are vital technology for building modern, interconnected systems and applications.

2. SOAP (Simple Object Access Protocol) API

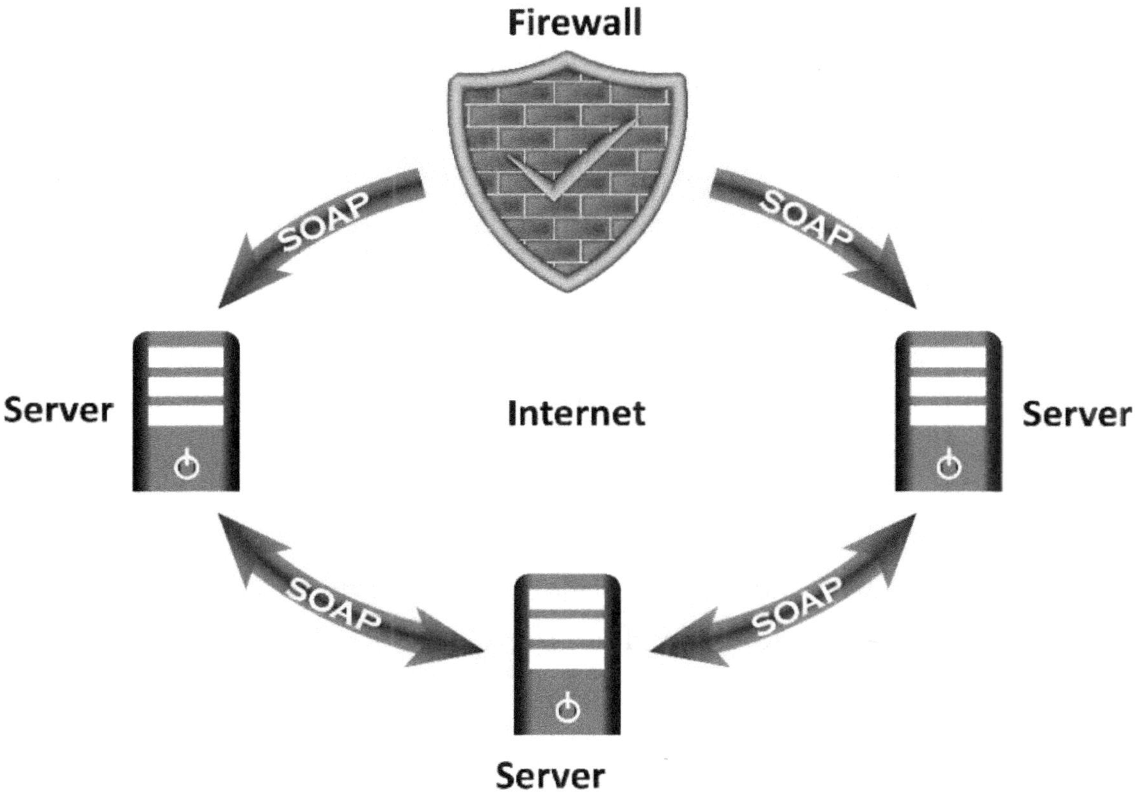

A popular kind of web API that enables the interchange of structured data and messages between various systems and applications is the Simple Object Access Protocol (SOAP) API. To interface with other applications or services, SOAP APIs rely on XML messaging and are based on protocols and specifications that specify how they should work.

SOAP APIs are based on a few fundamental principles that define how they should function and how they can be used. These principles include:

- **Messaging:** SOAP APIs are based on a messaging model, meaning they use XML messages to communicate between different systems or applications. These messages contain data or instructions that can be used to retrieve or modify data, execute a command, or perform another action.

- **Protocol Independence:** SOAP APIs are designed to be protocol-independent, which means they can be used with various protocols and transport mechanisms, including HTTP, SMTP, TCP, etc.

- **Extensibility:** Given their significant extensibility and adaptability, SOAP APIs can be tailored to match the unique requirements of various applications or systems. Namespaces let developers accomplish this by allowing them to create their distinctive features and attributes within a SOAP message.

- **Security:** SOAP APIs support a wide range of security features, including encryption, authentication, and authorization, which can help protect data and ensure that only authorized users or systems can access or modify it.

To use a SOAP API, a client application sends a SOAP request to the API, which returns a SOAP response in XML format. The request and response messages are structured using predefined rules and specifications, ensuring that different applications or systems can understand and process the messages.

SOAP APIs are used in various applications and systems, including web and mobile applications, enterprise systems, and cloud services. They are often preferred over other APIs for their security, reliability, and interoperability and are a key technology for building modern, interconnected systems and applications. However, SOAP APIs can be more complex and require more overhead than others, such as REST APIs, which may make them less suitable for some use cases.

3. GraphQL API

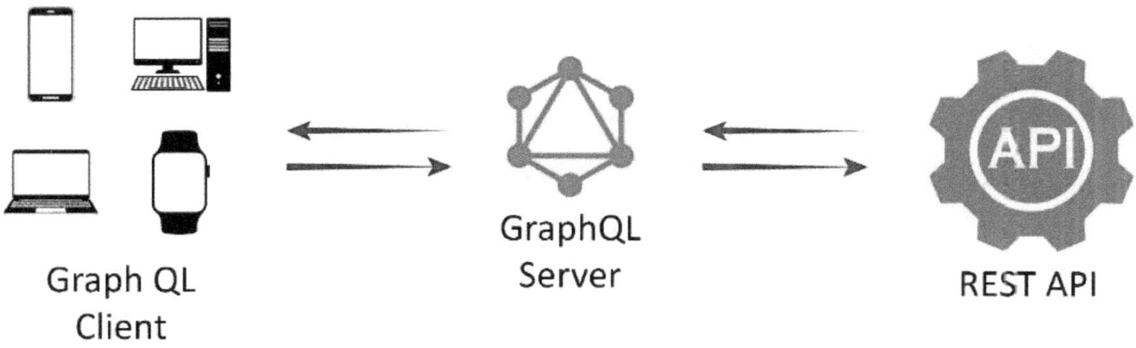

GraphQL is a relatively new type of web API that enables more efficient and flexible data retrieval and modification by providing a single endpoint for multiple resources. It was developed by Facebook in 2012 and was later open-sourced in 2015. Since then, GraphQL has gained popularity among developers and is widely used in web and mobile applications.

GraphQL APIs are based on a few fundamental principles that define how they should function and how they can be used. These principles include:

- **Schema-Driven:** GraphQL APIs are schema-driven, meaning they use a schema to define the data types that can be queried or modified. The schema defines the structure of the data and the relationships between different resources.

- **Query Language:** GraphQL APIs use a query language that enables clients to specify the exact data they need and receive only that data in response. The query language includes a set of operations, including queries, mutations, and subscriptions.

- **Strong Typing:** GraphQL APIs use strong typing, meaning the schema explicitly defines and enforces data types. This ensures that data is consistent and avoids clients needing to parse and validate data manually.

- **Hierarchical:** GraphQL APIs are hierarchical, meaning clients can specify a nested set of fields to retrieve data. This enables clients to retrieve complex data structures with a single query.

- **Single Endpoint:** GraphQL APIs provide a single endpoint for multiple resources, simplifying the API architecture and reducing the number of network requests required to retrieve data.

To use a GraphQL API, a client application sends a GraphQL query to the API, which returns a response in JSON format. The query specifies the exact data the client needs, and the answer only contains that data. The client can then parse and use the response data as required.

GraphQL APIs are used in various applications and systems, including web and mobile applications, e-commerce platforms, and social networks. They are often preferred over other APIs for their efficiency, flexibility, and ease of use. However, GraphQL APIs can be more complex to implement than different APIs. They may require more upfront planning and design to ensure the schema is appropriately defined and optimized for the use case.

4. RPC (Remote Procedure Call) API

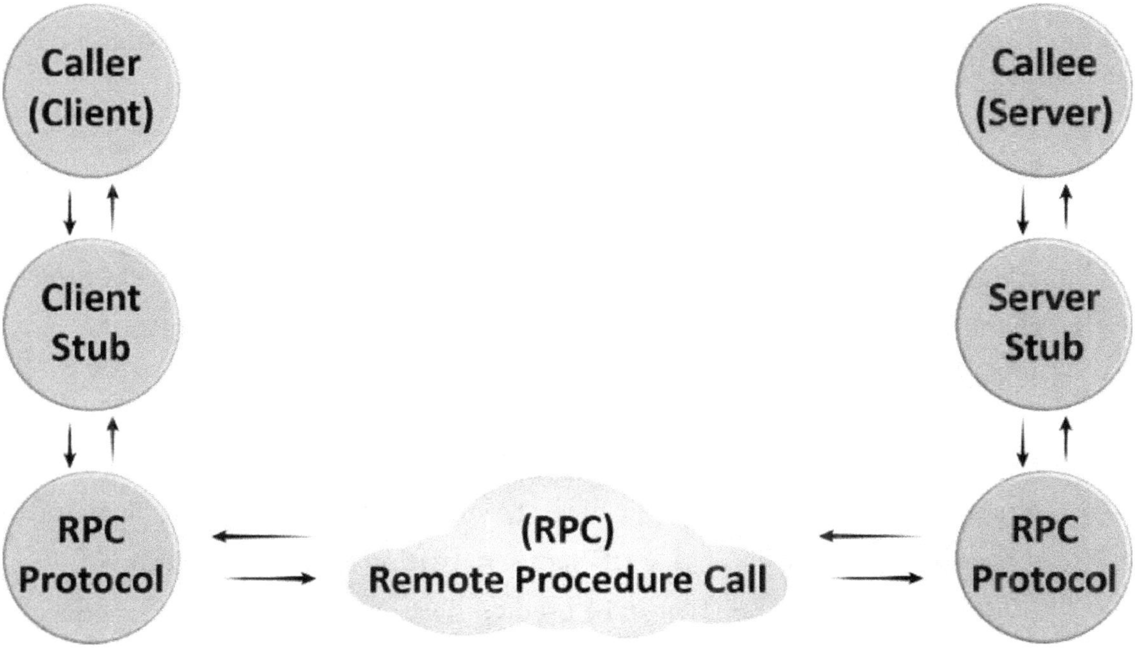

A Remote Procedure Call (RPC) is a communication protocol that enables a program running on one computer to call a function or procedure on a remote computer and receive the result as if running locally. RPC APIs are widely used in distributed computing environments where multiple systems must work together to achieve a common goal.

RPC APIs are based on a few fundamental principles that define how they should function and how they can be used. These principles include:

➢ **Procedural:** RPC APIs are procedural, which means that they enable a client application to call a function or procedure on a remote server and receive a response as if the function were running locally. The system can be any function defined on the server, taking input parameters and returning any output.

- **Transport Agnostic:** RPC APIs are transport agnostic, meaning they can be used with various transport mechanisms, including TCP, UDP, HTTP, etc. The transport mechanism used depends on the specific implementation of the RPC API.

- **Stub and Skeleton:** RPC APIs use a stub on the client side and a skeleton on the server side to enable communication between the client and server. The stub acts as a proxy for the client and makes the remote procedure call on behalf of the client. The skeleton receives the request on the server side and invokes the corresponding function or procedure.

- **Protocol Buffers:** RPC APIs often use a language- and platform-neutral data serialization format to define the message formats sent between the client and server. Protocol buffers enable efficient serialization and deserialization of complex data structures and can be used with various programming languages and platforms.

To use an RPC API, a client application first generates a request message, which includes the name of the function or procedure to call and any input parameters. The request message is then sent over the network to the server, which receives the message, extracts the function name and parameters, and executes the corresponding function or procedure. The server then generates a response message, which includes the result of the function or procedure call, and sends it back to the client over the network. RPC APIs are used in various applications and systems, including distributed systems, microservices, and cloud computing environments. They are often preferred over other APIs for their performance, reliability, and ease of use. However, RPC APIs can be more complex to implement than others and may require more overhead to set up and maintain the necessary infrastructure.

5. Webhooks

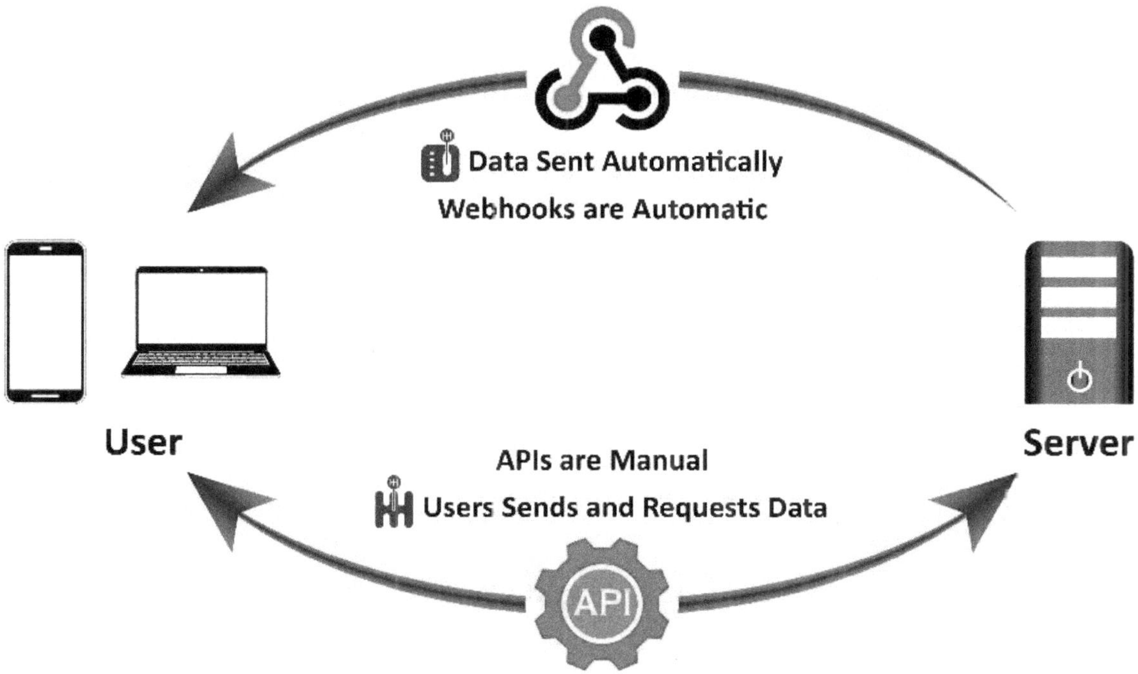

Webhooks are a type of API that enables real-time notifications and data synchronization between different systems or applications. Unlike traditional APIs, which require clients to poll the server for updates, webhooks allow the server to push updates to the client as they occur without needing the client to check for changes constantly.

Webhooks work by setting up a webhook endpoint on a client application, a URL the server can use to send updates. When an event occurs on the server that the client needs to be notified of, the server sends a POST request to the webhook endpoint, which includes information about the event.

The client application then receives the POST request, processes the data, and takes appropriate action based on the event. For example, a webhook might notify a client application when a user completes a purchase on an e-commerce website, allowing the client to update its database in real-time.

Webhooks are often used in conjunction with other types of APIs, such as REST APIs, to enable more efficient data synchronization and real-time updates. They are frequently utilized in many systems and applications, such as e-commerce platforms, social networks, and messaging programs.

Implementing webhooks requires a few key considerations:

- The client application must have a publicly accessible endpoint to receive POST requests.
- The server must be able to generate and send POST requests to the client endpoint.
- The client application must be able to process and handle the data included in the POST request.

Security is also an important consideration when implementing webhooks, as the client endpoint is publicly accessible and can be targeted by malicious actors. To mitigate security risks, webhook endpoints are recommended to use HTTPS encryption and that requests are validated using secure authentication mechanisms, such as OAuth or JSON Web Tokens.

Webhooks provide a simple and efficient way to enable real-time notifications and data synchronization between different systems or applications. They are widely used in various applications and techniques and can be implemented relatively easily using publicly accessible endpoints and secure authentication mechanisms.

6. WebSockets in API

The WebSockets protocol allows for creating a single, persistent connection that may be used to create a bi-directional communication channel between a client and a server. Unlike traditional HTTP connections, which are request-response based, WebSockets enable real-time, event-driven communication between clients and servers. WebSockets are commonly used in APIs to enable real-time notifications and data synchronization between different systems or applications. They are instrumental in applications that require frequent updates or low latency, such as chat applications, online gaming platforms, and financial trading systems.

The client makes an HTTP request to the server asking for an upgrade to the WebSocket protocol to create a WebSocket connection. If the server accepts the upgrade request, the client and server can communicate using the WebSocket protocol. Once the WebSocket connection is established, the client and server can send data to each other at any time without needing a request-response cycle. This is what enables real-time updates and notifications and allows the client and server to synchronize data in real-time. In addition to real-time notifications and data synchronization, WebSockets can implement other functionality types in APIs, such as chat rooms, multiplayer games, and collaborative document editing.

WebSockets are particularly useful in API development because they are easy to implement and can be used with various programming languages and platforms. Many popular programming languages, such as JavaScript, Python, and Ruby, have libraries and frameworks that make implementing WebSockets in API development easy.

Security is an important consideration when using WebSockets in API development. Compared to standard HTTP connections, they are more susceptible to assaults like distributed denial of service (DDoS) and denial of service (DoS) attacks because they use a persistent link. It is, therefore, essential to implement appropriate security measures, such as rate limiting, to prevent these types of attacks.

In conclusion, WebSockets is a powerful tool enabling real-time communication and data synchronization in APIs. They can be developed utilizing libraries and frameworks in several well-known programming languages and are widely used in various applications and systems. However, security considerations must be considered to prevent attacks and ensure the stability and reliability of the API.

7. Open APIs

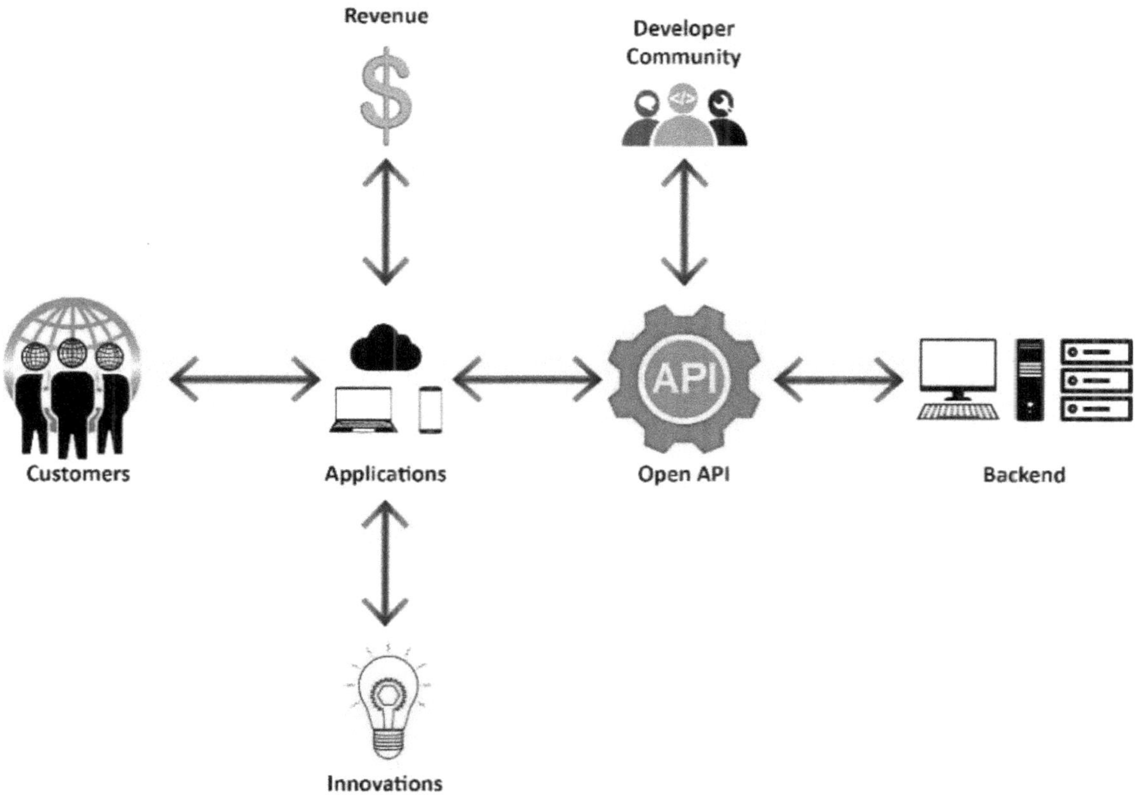

Open APIs, sometimes called public APIs, are frequently accessible to all users without the API provider's authorization or authorization. Open APIs are designed to be easily accessible and easy to use, making them an attractive option for developers and businesses looking to build integrations and connect their systems with external services.

Open APIs can provide access to a wide range of functionality, including data retrieval, storage, and real-time communication. Social networks, e-commerce platforms, and financial services are just a few of the systems and applications that frequently use them. Open APIs are typically accessed using HTTP requests, such as GET, POST, PUT, and DELETE, and are often designed using a RESTful architecture. This makes it easy to integrate with other systems and applications, as developers can use standard HTTP libraries and frameworks to interact with the API.

One of the key benefits of open APIs is their flexibility and versatility. They can provide access to a wide range of functionality and be customized and extended to meet the needs of specific use cases. This makes them popular for developers and businesses looking to build integrations and connect their systems with external services. Another benefit of open APIs is their ability to foster innovation and collaboration. By publicly making APIs available, API providers can encourage developers and businesses to build new applications and services that leverage them. This can lead to the creation of new business opportunities, as well as new ways of solving problems and delivering value to customers.

However, there are also some challenges associated with open APIs. Because they are publicly available, they can be vulnerable to attacks and abuse, such as denial of service (DoS) attacks, spamming, and unauthorized access. API providers must therefore implement appropriate security measures, such as authentication and rate limiting, to protect their APIs and ensure their stability and reliability.

Open APIs are a powerful tool for enabling integrations and connecting systems with external services. They provide a flexible and versatile way to access a wide range of functionality and can foster innovation and collaboration. However, API providers must also take appropriate security measures to protect their APIs and ensure their stability and reliability.

8. Partner APIs

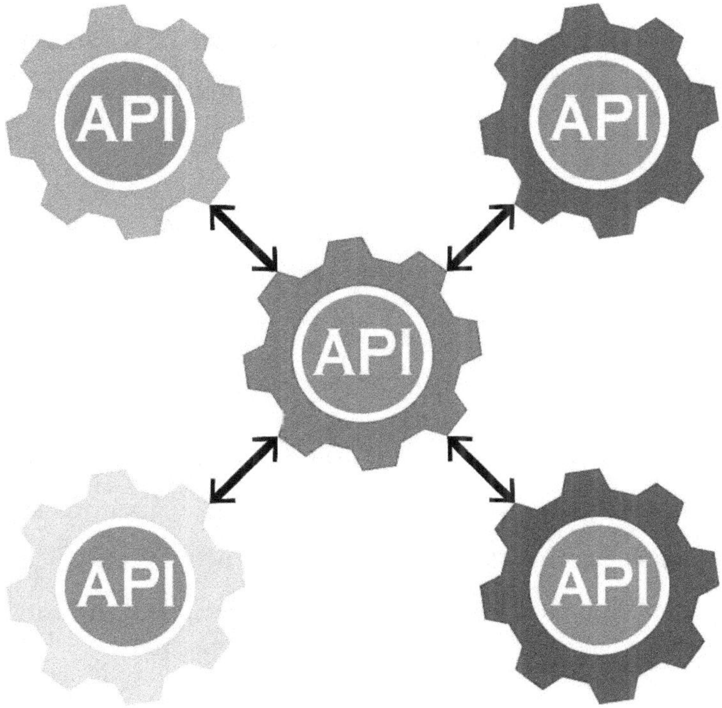

Partner APIs are APIs explicitly designed for use by external partners, such as vendors, suppliers, and resellers. These APIs allow partners to access and interact with data and functionality within a company's systems and applications, enabling them to collaborate more effectively and provide value to customers.

Partner APIs can provide access to a wide range of functionality, including product information, inventory management, order processing, and customer support. They are typically accessed using standard HTTP requests, such as GET, POST, PUT, and DELETE, and may be designed using a RESTful architecture.

One of its key advantages is partner APIs' capacity to simplify business procedures and enhance cooperation between businesses and their partners. Companies may reduce the time and effort needed to manage relationships and collaborate on projects by giving partners immediate access to data and functionality within their systems and applications.

Partner APIs can also help companies expand their reach and grow their business by allowing partners to integrate their products and services with the company's offerings. This can lead to the creation of new business opportunities and revenue streams, as well as improved customer satisfaction and loyalty.

Another benefit of partner APIs is their ability to provide granular access controls and permissions. API providers can use authentication and authorization mechanisms to ensure that partners can only access the data and functionality needed to perform their specific tasks. This helps to protect sensitive data and prevent unauthorized access and abuse. However, there are also some challenges associated with partner APIs. Because they are designed for external use, they may require more robust security measures and monitoring than internal APIs. API providers must also ensure their APIs are scalable and performant, as partner usage can fluctuate significantly based on business needs.

Partner APIs are used for enabling collaboration and streamlining business processes between companies and their partners. They provide a way to access and interact with data and functionality within a company's systems and applications and can help to expand business opportunities and improve customer satisfaction. However, API providers must also take appropriate security and performance measures to ensure the stability and reliability of their APIs.

9. Internal APIs

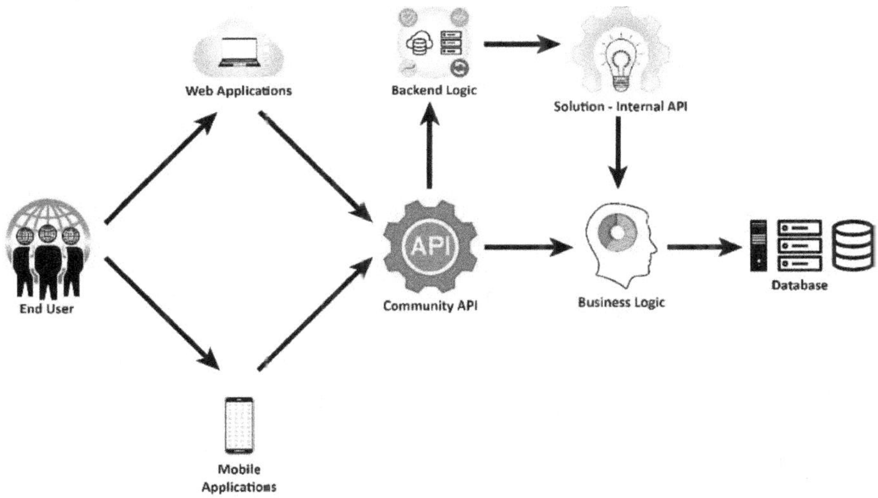

Internal or private APIs are designed for use within an organization or company. These APIs enable communication and data exchange between different systems, applications, and services within the organization and are not publicly accessible.

Internal APIs can provide access to a wide range of functionality, including data retrieval, storage, and real-time communication. They are commonly used in various industries, including healthcare, finance, and manufacturing, to facilitate communication and collaboration between departments and systems. Internal APIs may be created using a RESTful architecture and are often accessed using standard HTTP queries like GET, POST, PUT, and DELETE. They are often integrated into internal systems and applications, such as enterprise resource planning (ERP) software, customer relationship management (CRM) systems, and supply chain management (SCM) systems.

One of the critical benefits of internal APIs is their ability to improve productivity and efficiency within an organization. Internal APIs offer a standardized method for different systems and applications to send and receive data, saving the effort and time required to manage and coordinate numerous processes and workflows.

Internal APIs can also help to improve data accuracy and consistency by ensuring that all systems and applications within an organization are accessing the same data sources and using consistent data formats and standards. This can help prevent errors and reduce the risk of data duplication and inconsistency risk.

Another benefit of internal APIs is their ability to provide granular access controls and permissions. API providers can use authentication and authorization mechanisms to ensure that only authorized users and systems have access to the data and functionality provided by the API. This helps to protect sensitive data and prevent unauthorized access and abuse.

However, there are also some challenges associated with internal APIs. Because they are designed for use within an organization, they may not be as flexible or versatile as public APIs. They may require more complex authentication and authorization mechanisms to ensure security and access control. Developing and maintaining internal APIs can also require significant resources and expertise, which may be a challenge for smaller organizations.

Internal APIs are often used for communication and data exchange between organizational systems and applications. They can help to improve productivity, efficiency, and data accuracy while providing granular access controls and permissions to protect sensitive data. However, API providers must also address the unique challenges associated with internal APIs, including security, access control, and resource requirements.

Using APIs

Using APIs typically involves a few key steps, including:

1. **Identifying the API**

   The first step in using an API is identifying the API that provides the data or functionality needed. This may involve searching a directory of APIs or working with a provider directly.

2. **Obtaining access**

   Once the API has been identified, the next step is obtaining access. This may involve registering for an API key or obtaining OAuth credentials.

3. **Making Requests**

   With access obtained, the next step is to make requests to the API using the appropriate protocol and request/response formats.

4. **Handling Responses**

   Finally, responses from the API should be handled appropriately within the application, which may involve parsing JSON or XML data, error handling, and data validation.

API Testing

Application Programming Interfaces (APIs) allow different software systems to communicate and exchange data. Due to the rising popularity of cloud-based apps and microservices architecture in recent years, API usage has increased tremendously. The process of creating software and assuring its quality must include API testing. API testing involves verifying an API's functionality, performance, reliability, and in this case, security. API testing can be performed at different levels, including unit, integration, system, and acceptance. API testing can be done manually or using automated tools.

API testing involves testing the following aspects of an API:

1. **Functionality Testing**

   This involves testing the API's functionality to ensure it meets the requirements and specifications. It includes testing the response of the API to different input parameters, testing error handling, and testing the API's behavior in different scenarios.

2. **Performance Testing**

   This involves testing the API's performance to ensure that it can handle many requests and that response times are within acceptable limits. It includes testing the API's response time, throughput, and concurrency.

3. **Security Testing**

   This involves testing the API's security to ensure it is secure against common attacks such as injection attacks, Cross-Site Scripting (XSS) attacks, and Cross-Site

Request Forgery (CSRF) attacks. It includes testing authentication and authorization mechanisms, data encryption, and data validation.

Advantages of API Testing

1. Faster Testing

API testing can automate the testing process, which saves time and effort compared to manual testing. Faster feedback on modifications and updates is possible thanks to the speed and repetition of automated tests.

2. Improved Accuracy

API testing can provide more accurate results than manual testing. Automatic testing can find problems that manual testing would miss since it is less prone to human mistakes.

3. Increased Test Coverage

API testing can test many scenarios and use cases, increasing the overall test coverage. This helps ensure that all API parts are thoroughly tested and that any issues are identified before deployment.

4. Better Collaboration

API testing provides a centralized testing platform for better collaboration between developers and testers. Test results can be easily shared and reviewed, and issues can be tracked and resolved more efficiently.

5. Cost-Effective

API testing can save costs by detecting issues early in the development process, which reduces the cost of fixing defects later. It also reduces the time and effort required for manual testing, which can result in cost savings.

API Testing Challenges

1. **Complexity**

   APIs can be complex and may have several endpoints and methods, making testing challenging. API testing requires a thorough understanding of the API and its functionality.

2. **Technical Skills**

   API testing requires specialized skills and knowledge of programming languages and tools. Testers may need experience with scripting, coding, and automation tools.

3. **Security**

   APIs can be a target for security attacks so API testing must include security testing to ensure the API is secure against common attacks.

4. **Dependency on Other Systems**

   APIs often depend on other systems, such as databases or web services, and testing the API may also require testing these dependencies.

5. **Testing Environments**

   API testing may require different testing environments, such as staging or production, which can be challenging to set up and maintain.

While API testing provides several advantages, including faster testing, improved accuracy, and increased test coverage, it also comes with challenges such as complexity, technical skills, security, dependency on other systems, and testing environments. Testers must thoroughly understand the API and its dependencies and be familiar with the tools and techniques required for API testing.

Types of API Testing

1. Unit Testing

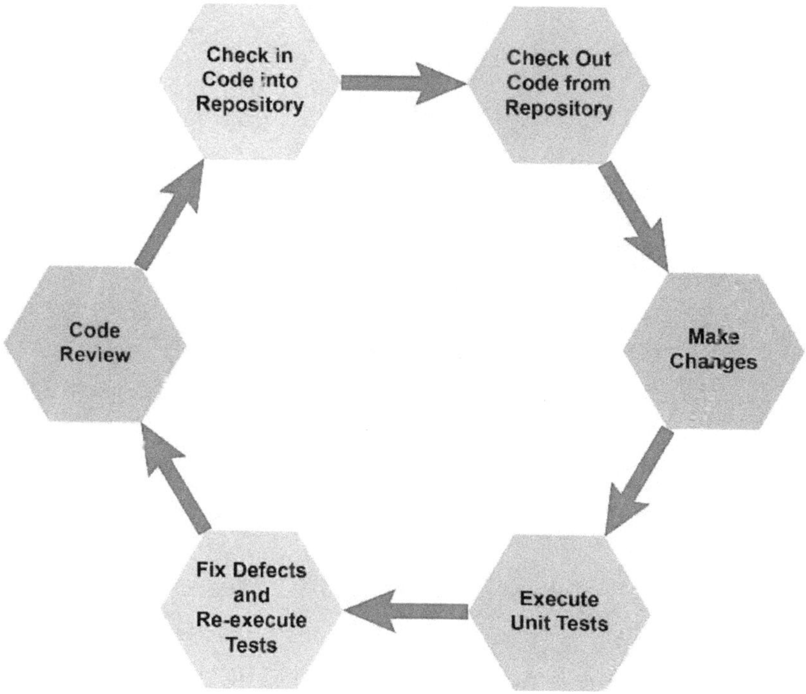

Unit testing is testing that concentrates on testing isolated instances of specific API units or components. Unit testing is used to ensure that each unit of code is functioning as intended and adheres to its requirements. Developers create test cases covering various API functionalities, including input validation, response validation, error handling, and security. These tests can be automated to ensure that the API consistently produces the expected results, regardless of the environment or conditions under which it is used.

To implement unit testing in API, developers use testing frameworks such as JUnit, NUnit, or Mocha, which provide tools for creating and executing test cases.

Developers also use mocking libraries such as Mockito or Sinon to create mock objects that simulate the behavior of external dependencies, allowing the API to be tested in isolation.

2. Functional Testing

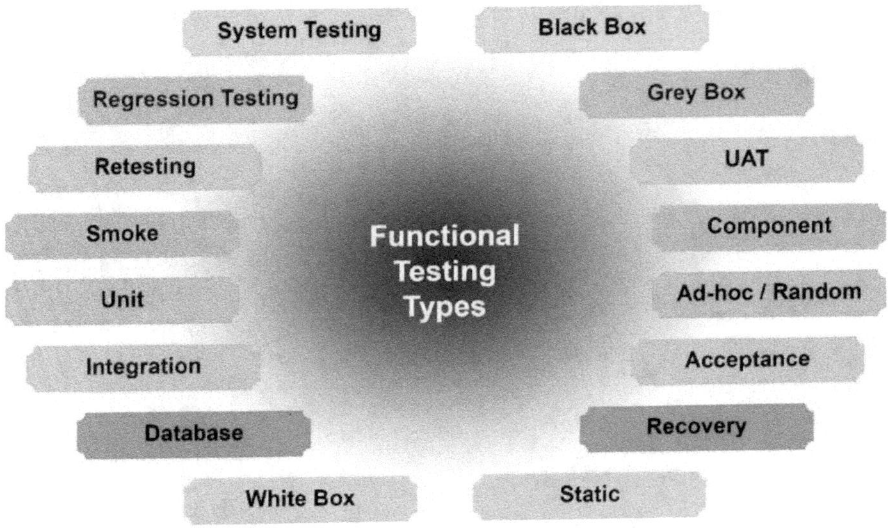

Functional testing tests the functional behavior of the API by verifying that it behaves as expected for different inputs and conditions. This type of testing is crucial because it ensures that the API meets the requirements and specifications set out in its design.

To implement functional API testing, developers use frameworks that provide tools for creating and executing test cases. They also use Postman or Swagger UI tools to create and execute API requests and verify their responses. Automated testing tools like Selenium or Puppeteer can test API integration with web applications.

3. Load Testing

Load testing tests the performance of the API under different load conditions to ensure that it can handle the expected amount of traffic and requests. This type of testing is essential for APIs that are expected to handle large volumes of data or requests. To implement load testing in API, developers use tools such as JMeter, Gatling, or Locust, which simulate different load conditions and generate reports on the API's performance metrics. Developers can also use cloud-based load-testing services like LoadRunner or BlazeMeter to test the API's scalability and performance under different traffic loads.

4. Security Testing

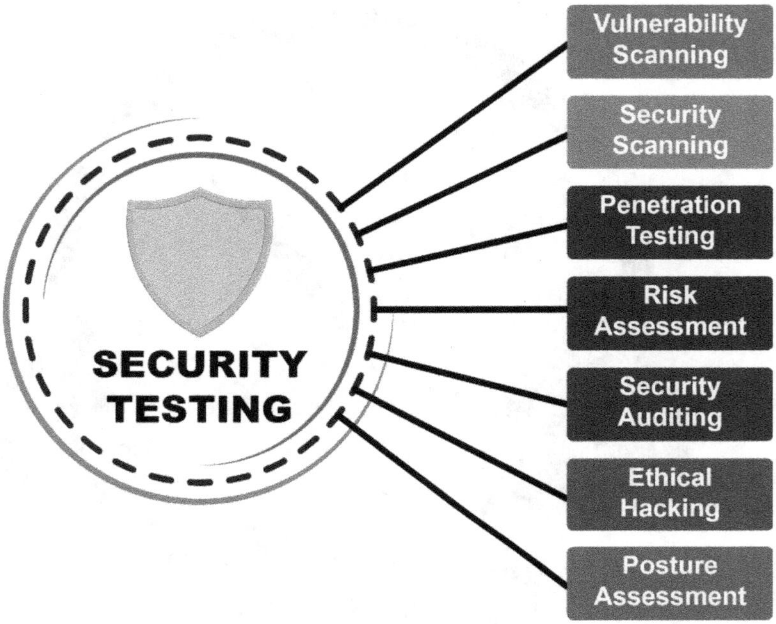

Security testing tests the API's security features and ensures they function correctly to protect against potential vulnerabilities. This type of testing is essential for APIs that handle sensitive or confidential data, such as financial or personal information. To implement security testing in API, developers use security testing tools such as OWASP ZAP, Burp Suite, or Nessus, which simulate different attack scenarios and identify security vulnerabilities in the API. Developers can also use static code analysis tools such as SonarQube or Checkmarx to detect and fix security issues in the API's source code but manual testing by security professionals is always recommended.

5. Interoperability Testing

Interoperability testing tests the API's compatibility with different operating systems, browsers, and other software to ensure it can function correctly in different environments. This type of testing is essential for APIs that are expected to work with various software applications or platforms.

Developers use frameworks that support cross-platform testing to implement API interoperability testing, such as Appium or Test Complete. Developers can also use cloud-based testing services such as Sauce Labs or BrowserStack to test the API's compatibility with different browsers, operating systems, and devices.

6. Penetration Testing

Penetration testing involves simulating a real-world attack on the API to identify vulnerabilities and weaknesses in its security. This type of testing is essential for APIs that handle sensitive or confidential data and ensures they are protected against potential cyberthreats.

To implement penetration testing in API, developers use specialized penetration testing tools such as Metasploit or Nmap, which simulate different attack scenarios and identify vulnerabilities in the API's security. Developers can also use third-party security services such as Hacker One or Bugcrowd to conduct security assessments and identify potential vulnerabilities in the API.

Technical Aspects

1. API Documentation

API documentation is essential for API testing as it provides a clear understanding of the API's design, functionality, and expected behavior. Developers should ensure the API documentation is up-to-date, accurate, and comprehensive to support testing activities.

2. Test Automation:

API testing should be automated wherever possible to reduce manual effort, increase testing coverage, and improve test accuracy. Developers should use testing frameworks, scripting languages, and automation tools to create and execute automated test cases.

3. Mocking and Stubs

Developers should use mocking and stubbing techniques to simulate the behavior of external dependencies and reduce the complexity of testing. Mocking and stubbing allow developers to isolate the API from external dependencies and focus on testing its behavior in isolation.

4. Performance and Load Testing

Performance and load testing are important aspects of API testing. Developers should use specialized tools and techniques to simulate load conditions and identify performance bottlenecks.

5. Security Testing

Security testing is critical for APIs that handle sensitive or confidential data. Developers should use specialized tools and techniques to identify vulnerabilities and weaknesses in the API's security.

Implementation Considerations

1. Test Coverage

Developers should ensure they cover all the API's critical functional and non-functional aspects in their test cases. Test cases should cover different inputs, use cases, and scenarios to ensure the API behaves as expected in other conditions.

2. Integration with Development Process

API testing should be integrated with the development process to ensure that issues are identified and resolved early in the development cycle. Developers should use continuous integration and delivery (CI/CD) tools and techniques to automate the testing process and provide rapid feedback on changes to the API.

3. Environment Management

Developers should ensure access to a suitable testing environment that mirrors the production environment as closely as possible. The testing environment should be isolated from other domains, and developers should use virtualization and containerization techniques to ensure consistency and reproducibility of testing results.

4. Collaboration and Communication

API testing requires close collaboration and communication between developers, testers, and stakeholders. Developers should ensure that they have clear and effective communication channels with stakeholders. Testing should be integrated into the agile development process to ensure that issues are identified and resolved quickly.

5. Test Data Management

Developers should ensure they have access to suitable test data that represents the real-world use of the API. Test data should be clean, representative, and diverse, and developers should use data generation and management tools to ensure consistency and accuracy of testing results.

API testing requires careful consideration and planning to ensure that the API meets its intended purpose and delivers a high-quality user experience. Developers should focus on the technical aspects of API testing, such as test automation, mocking, and security testing, and consider the implementation considerations, such as test coverage, environment management, and collaboration and communication, to ensure successful API testing.

API Testing Tools

API testing tools and frameworks are essential for developers and testers to perform effective API testing. These tools provide various features and functionalities to create, execute, and analyze API test cases. This section will discuss some of the most popular API testing tools and frameworks.

Postman

Postman is among the most widely used API testing tools by programmers and testers worldwide. It offers a user-friendly interface for creating and executing API test cases, and its features include automated testing, collaboration, version control, and documentation. It also integrates with tools and services like CI/CD, monitoring, and testing frameworks.

Advantages of Postman:

- user-friendly interface that is easy to use
- supports multiple data formats and protocols
- offers collaboration and sharing features for team testing
- allows for easy automation of test cases
- provides detailed reporting and analysis features

SoapUI

SoapUI is a widely used API testing tool that offers powerful features for testing SOAP and REST APIs. Its features include automated testing, data-driven testing, assertion creation, security testing, and performance testing. SoapUI integrates with tools and services like CI/CD, JIRA, and Jenkins.

Advantages of SoapUI:

- supports multiple protocols and data formats
- offers a wide range of features, including testing, mocking, and load testing
- provides detailed reporting and analysis features
- integrates well with other tools and frameworks

- supports both functional and security testing

JMeter

JMeter is a widely used load-testing tool offering API testing capabilities. It supports protocols such as HTTP, FTP, and JDBC and offers features such as automated testing, assertion creation, data-driven testing, and performance testing. JMeter also integrates with other tools and services like CI/CD, Jenkins, and Grafana.

Advantages of JMeter:

- offers powerful load testing capabilities
- supports multiple protocols and data formats
- provides detailed reporting and analysis features
- open-source and free to use
- integrates well with other tools and frameworks

Swagger

Swagger is an open-source tool used for API testing, documentation, and design. It supports various programming languages and data formats, including YAML and JSON.

Advantages of Swagger:

- offers robust documentation and design features in addition to testing
- supports multiple programming languages and data formats
- provides detailed reporting and analysis features

- integrates well with other tools and frameworks.
- easy to learn and use

Assertible

This cloud-based API testing tool offers a simple and intuitive interface for creating and executing API test cases. It supports automated testing, integration with CI/CD tools, and custom reporting features. Assertible also provides a webhook quality for integrating with other devices and services.

Advantages of Assertible:

- offers real-time monitoring and notifications
- provides detailed reporting and analysis features
- integrates with various continuous integration and deployment tools
- easy to learn and use
- includes support for webhooks and integrations with other tools

Rest-Assured

Rest-Assured is a Java-based library used for testing RESTful APIs. It provides an easy-to-use DSL (Domain Specific Language) for writing API tests.

Advantages of Rest-Assured:

- provides an easy-to-use DSL for writing API tests
- supports various authentication protocols and data formats
- integrates with multiple testing frameworks and tools

- offers support for BDD testing
- provides detailed reporting and analysis features

Karate

Karate is an open-source tool used for testing RESTful APIs. It provides a simple syntax for writing API tests and supports various data formats, including JSON and XML.

Advantages of Karate:

- provides a simple syntax for writing API tests
- supports various data formats and protocols
- provides support for BDD testing
- integrates well with other tools and frameworks
- offers support for parallel testing

HttpMaster

HttpMaster is a professional API testing tool for functional, performance, and load testing of APIs. It supports various data formats and authentication protocols, including OAuth and JWT.

Advantages of HttpMaster:

- offers a wide range of features for API testing, including functional, performance, and load testing
- supports various data formats and authentication protocols

- provides detailed reporting and analysis features
- offers a free version for basic testing needs
- integrates well with other tools and frameworks

Tricentis Tosca

Tricentis Tosca is a test automation tool that supports API and functional and regression testing. It provides an intuitive user interface for creating and managing API tests.

Advantages of Tricentis Tosca:

- provides a unified platform for API testing along with functional and regression testing
- offers a user-friendly interface for creating and managing tests
- supports various protocols and data formats

Katalon Studio

Katalon Studio is a test automation tool that supports API and web and mobile testing. It provides a built-in API testing feature that supports various data formats and authentication protocols.

Advantages of Katalon Studio:

- provides a built-in API testing feature that supports various data formats and authentication protocols
- supports both web and mobile testing
- offers a user-friendly interface for creating and managing tests

API testing frameworks and tools are essential for assuring the consistency and quality of APIs. Developers and testers can choose from various devices and frameworks based on their needs and requirements. Popular tools such as Postman, SoapUI, Rest-Assured, Karate, JMeter, Newman, and Assertible provide a range of features and functionalities to create, execute, and analyze API test cases.

Best Practices for API Testing

API testing is an important step in the Software Development Life Cycle (SDLC) as it helps ensure your API is functional, performant, and secure.

1. Test for Functionality

One of the primary objectives of API testing is to ensure that the API functions correctly. Therefore, testing for expected and unexpected input and output, error handling, and response codes is essential. API testing should also cover all the endpoints and methods available in the API.

2. Test for Performance

Performance testing should be essential to API testing, as it helps determine how the API behaves under load. Load testing, stress testing, and endurance testing are examples of performance testing. Load testing simulates real-world traffic to the API, while stress testing pushes the API beyond its limits. Endurance testing helps verify that the API can handle sustained loads over time.

3. Test for Security

APIs are vulnerable to several security risks, including SQL injection, Cross-Site Scripting (XSS), and Man-in-the-Middle (MitM) attacks. Therefore, testing for security vulnerabilities is essential to ensure your API is secure. Security testing should cover authentication, authorization, input validation, and output encoding.

4. **Use Automation**

   Manual testing is time-consuming and prone to errors. Therefore, automation is crucial to save time, reduce errors, and increase efficiency. Automation tools like Postman, SoapUI, and JMeter can help automate API testing.

5. **Test with Different Data Types**

   It's essential to test your API with different data types, such as integers, strings, and objects, to ensure that the API behaves correctly and can handle various data formats. It's also essential to test for data validation, data transformation, and data serialization.

6. **Use Mock Data**

   Mock data can be helpful in API testing to simulate different scenarios, such as error conditions and edge cases, without using live data. Mock data can help you test your API without relying on external systems like databases or other APIs.

7. **Continuous Testing**

   Continuous testing involves running automated tests as part of the development process to detect issues early and ensure that changes don't break existing functionality. Continuous testing can be achieved by integrating API testing into the Continuous Integration and Continuous Deployment (CI/CD) pipeline.

8. Document Your Tests

Documenting your tests helps to track changes, identify issues, and improve collaboration among team members. Documentation should include test cases, test data, and test results.

APIs are vital for modern software development but come with potential security risks. To mitigate these risks, following API security best practices and implementing proper testing measures is essential. API testing should cover functionality, performance, security, and integrations and be automated where possible to save time and reduce the risk of human error. Other best practices include using mock data, testing with different data types, and continuous testing to ensure that APIs remain secure and functional as code changes. Overall, by prioritizing API security and following best practices for API testing, developers can create robust and secure APIs that meet user needs and protect against potential threats.

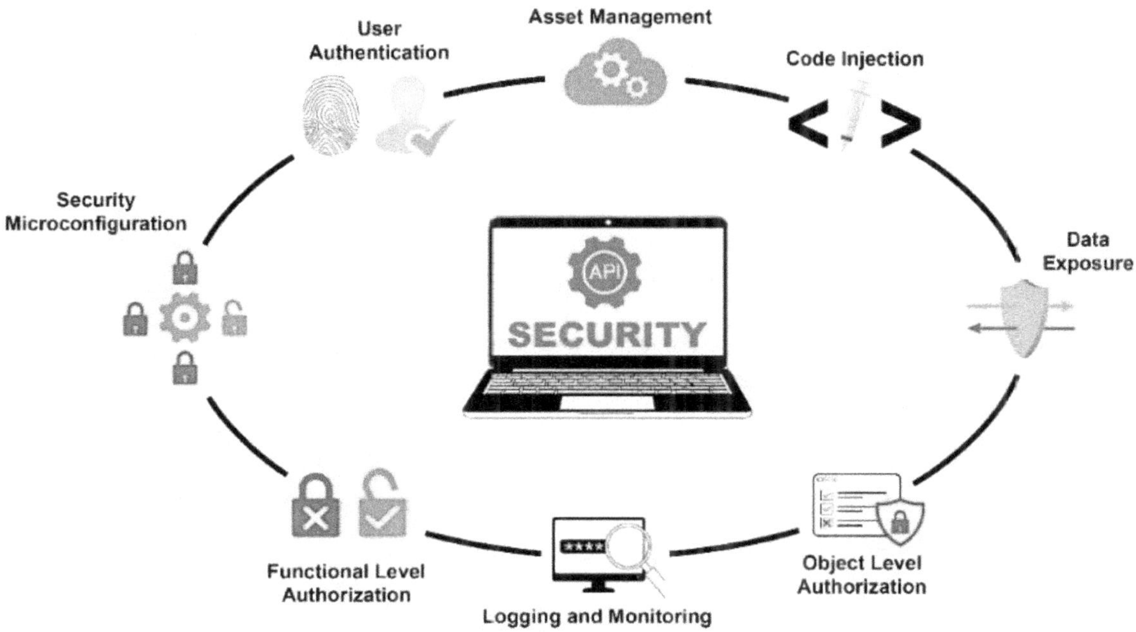

Best Practices for API Security

With the increase in API usage, there is a corresponding increase in security risks, making it essential to implement best practices for API security to ensure that APIs are secure and protected from malicious attacks. Best practices for API security include implementing authentication and authorization, encryption, rate limiting, etc. By following these best practices, developers can build secure and reliable APIs that are ready to be used to integrate different software applications and systems.

1. Authentication and Authorization

APIs should implement a strong authentication and authorization mechanism to ensure that only authorized users can access the API. This can be done by implementing OAuth2 or JWT-based authentication. The API should also validate the user's authorization level before allowing access to sensitive data or operations.

2. **Encryption**

   All data transmitted over the API should be encrypted using industry-standard encryption protocols such as TLS, and this ensures that unauthorized users cannot intercept and read the data.

3. **Rate Limiting**

   APIs should implement rate limiting to prevent overloading and abuse of the API. This can be accomplished by restricting the number of requests submitted in a specific time frame.

4. **Input Validation and Sanitization**

   APIs should validate and sanitize all inputs received from the user to prevent injection attacks such as SQL injection and cross-site scripting. This can be done by implementing input validation and sanitization techniques such as data type validation, parameter binding, and input length validation.

5. **Error Handling**

   APIs should handle errors gracefully and not reveal sensitive information in error messages. Error messages should be logged and monitored for security purposes.

6. Audit Logging and Monitoring

APIs should implement audit logging and monitoring to track all API activity. This can be done by logging all API requests and responses, monitoring suspicious activity, and alerting administrators in case of security breaches.

7. Versioning

APIs should implement versioning to ensure that changes to the API do not break existing integrations.

This can be done by versioning the API endpoints and providing documentation for the changes made in each version.

API security is a critical aspect of software development where implementing the best practices help ensure that APIs are secure and protected from malicious attacks. By following these best practices, developers can build secure and reliable APIs that can be used to integrate different software applications and systems.

Looking into Web Proxies

A proxy server is defined as a system or router that provides a link between users and the internet, playing a significant role in preventing unauthorized access to private networks. It is often referred to as an "intermediary" server due to its function of bridging the gap between end-users and the web pages they access. When a computer establishes a connection to the internet, it utilizes an IP address, which can be likened to a street address for a home. This address directs incoming data to the correct location while also labeling outgoing data with a return address, enabling other devices to authenticate the source. Thus, a proxy server operates as a computer on the internet, equipped with its own unique IP address.

A company employs a web proxy server for better performance and cybersecurity, including hiding internal IP addresses and caching content for faster data transfers and less bandwidth utilization. Corporations can use a web proxy server to block websites from being downloaded onto their internal network. These servers act as a connection between client devices and the web. Although they are typically utilized in professional situations, some cloud hosting firms provide web proxy servers for users with lower bandwidth who require greater online bandwidth utilization. We can also define a web proxy server as a web server that acts as a gateway between a client application, a browser, and the real server. It requests for the actual server on behalf of the client or sometimes fulfills the claim itself.

Why Should You Use a Web Proxy?

Web proxy servers have two primary purposes: cybersecurity and performance. If the server caches huge files like images and media, businesses that use web proxies save money on bandwidth. A web proxy is often inexpensive to construct, making it a cost-effective IT device.

Anonymizing Internal IP Addresses

In the modern workplace, having access to the internet is essential, but granting employees open, unrestricted access to it exposes the business to several risks. The originating IP address is recorded on the server whenever staff members connect to a server under the control of an attacker. Attackers may utilize this IP address, typically a router IP address, to launch a denial-of-service (DoS) attack. Additionally, it may reveal to the attacker the identities of your employees accessing the website, enabling more specialized attacks like malware.

A web proxy server prevents an attacker from accessing the corporate router's outgoing IP address because the IP address displayed in weblogs is that of the web proxy. The internal router is much more vulnerable to a DoS assault, but one against the proxy server is still a possibility and considerably less risky.

It's also essential to anonymize outgoing IP addresses when doing sensitive tasks online. For instance, an internal IP address that links back to the researchers would not be disclosed if law enforcement looked into a website. An anonymous web proxy from a third party would be helpful for investigations and other internet activities.

Caching and Performance Benefits

The browser stores cached copies of files in local storage when a user accesses a website in their browser. The browser searches the cache for files and uses them to show content the next time the user views the website. Both the web admin and the user can disable caching. However, most people have their browsers set up to use browser cache rather than download new files each visit to a website by using cached content, which makes an excellent performance to website browsing.

Imagine a network connection of 1,000 users who regularly visit the same website. Users must consume the bandwidth to browse the website and download cached information. However, what if the content could be downloaded once and dispersed among all 1,000 user devices? If all 1,000 personnel remained connected to the proxy server, it would download files, store them locally, and then transfer the cached content to user devices when they view a frequently visited website.

Performance is the first advantage of employing a web proxy to cache material. Users do not have to download files again because the device already has the proxy server's cached content. Cost savings are the second advantage. The majority of corporate internet connections bill based on the monthly bandwidth used. Users who download cached content do not consume the same bandwidth as those who download files directly from the origin server.

Blocking Unwanted Content

Corporations must provide internet connectivity for personnel, but phishing and malware threaten the data's security. A web proxy server is one of the strategies used to control the content on user devices. Users can configure a web proxy to block websites from specific IP addresses or domains.

The company must either engage a third-party service or get a list of notified domains to block content. The web proxy server alerts users that content is blocked when accessing a secured domain. Administrators can detect frequently prohibited items by looking at a log of the access request created.

Risks of Using a Proxy Server

A new website proxy server has a few drawbacks, but using public services available to everyone has some risks. These dangers are eliminated if corporations utilize network restrictions to require users only to use the authorized proxy server. Network administrators can lock web browser configurations using domain controls like Database.

Unrestrained proxy servers are the most significant risk. Attackers use a web proxy server to trick users into connecting and revealing sensitive information. A web proxy gives all traffic access to the server administrator. If this traffic is not encrypted, it may result in account takeover or identity theft. The user's data is logged on the web proxy server in exchange for an anonymized IP address.

Though utilizing a web proxy is frequently done for privacy-related reasons, no data that passes through the server as an intermediary is ever private. Users should be aware that attackers can access their browser history and should only use free proxy servers for non-sensitive traffic. Users may be attacked by various assaults, such as phishing, based on their search history.

Most public free web proxy servers do not use encryption, which means that all traffic can be read in clear text on the server and as it passes across the internet. This issue is not a threat to simple browsing and traffic that is not sensitive. Still, users should never connect to a public free web proxy while authenticating into sites that contain sensitive data, such as banking accounts or e-commerce accounts with stored payment methods.

Types of Proxy Servers

Though a website can be installed in a firm to safeguard internal users, public proxy servers enable varying degrees of privacy. Understanding the various kinds of proxy servers is essential if you want to know what information the web proxy owner and website host server will have access to. Connecting to a proxy server doesn't encrypt IP addresses and offers very little privacy.

1. Transparent Proxy

The least private proxy server is a transparent one. The target website receives your user's IP address over a direct proxy connection. The only advantage of a transparent proxy is that it will improve performance by caching material. They can be utilized to restrict harmful content as well. Public internet service providers like libraries and educational institutions use transparent proxies.

To send the original IP to a specified web host, web proxies employ several request headers. "Forwarded" and "X-Forwarded-For" are the two most typical. Test your transparent proxy to see if it forwards your original IP address before using it to browse a website.

2. Anonymous Pr

2. Anonymous Proxy

An anonymous proxy is ideal for non-critical traffic if the user wants to remain anonymous while surfing the web. The administrator of the targeted website can identify an anonymous proxy, but it won't send the user's IP address to the host. Users can browse the web fully anonymously due to this server.

3. Distorting Proxy

A distorted proxy goes beyond an anonymous proxy by sending a falsified IP address to the desired website. This server will make the user appear from a different location, hiding the user's geolocation from the website administrator.

4. High Anonymity Proxy

A high anonymity proxy is the most anonymous of all web proxies. High-anonymity web proxy servers used by the Tor network. These web proxy services provide encryption, hide the user's IP from malicious website owners, and frequently modify the outgoing IP. Users retain total privacy as a result, including geographical encryption.

Software for web proxy servers is accessible and reasonably priced, and it may be used on a corporate network as well as a small home or business network. The proceeding are some instances of server software that can be used to host any web proxy:

- Apache
- Wingate
- Nginx
- Privoxy

- Squid
- Varnish
- Internet Information Services (IIS) (Windows server operating systems come with this.)
- Ziproxy
- HAProxy
- Tinyproxy
- Rabbit
- Polipo

What Is a VPN?

A VPN is a tool that allows you to protect your connection while you browse the internet. With a VPN (Virtual Private Network), you can hide your IP and encrypt all the data you send or receive over the internet so that it is inaccessible to third parties trying to intercept your connection. This allows you to browse privately and keep your IP out of the reach of potential cyberattacks.

Types of VPNs

There are several types of VPNs, and it can be hard to understand how they differ. However, VPNs fall into one of two categories, which makes it easier to figure out which VPN is right for you.

1. Remote Access VPN

A remote access VPN routes your connection through a secure remote server that permits you to establish a private connection. Additionally, it encrypts data to secure it.

Remote access VPNs are the most popular options for personal use, and additionally, they form the infrastructure of commercial VPN services. To use a remote access VPN, you typically have to install the VPN software on your computer and log in to secure your internet connection. One of the key advantages of a VPN with a remote access model is its simplicity. This kind of VPN is the best option for personal usage because it is easy enough for beginners to utilize. However, scaled operations or businesses typically cannot access remote access VPNs.

2. Site-to-Site VPN

Site-to-site VPNs allow multiple users to access each other's resources from fixed locations. For example, if you're working in a company with office locations in various cities, they might use a site-to-site VPN to secure company data.

Site-to-site VPNs secure data by ensuring all local area connections (LAN) connect to the same vast area network (WAN). All the offices are connected, and the data they share is encrypted and protected by the VPN.

Site-to-site VPNs encrypt all gateways, which means users don't need to download VPN software to secure their data. Once a user logs into the company network, the VPN goes to work.

There are two types of site-to-site VPN services:

- Intranet VPN
- Extranet VPN

Intranet VPNs are used when one company wants to connect multiple locations securely, while Extranet VPNs connect multiple companies so they can securely share data and resources.

With site-to-site, the benefits of a VPN include security, efficiency, and scalability, which makes them ideal for corporations.

Considerations Before Using A VPN

If you're sold on the benefits of a VPN, the next step is choosing the right option. Before using a VPN, keep these things in mind:

1. **Device compatibility**

   VPNs can be used on laptops, tablets, mobile devices, and operating systems. Before you purchase VPN services, check to see if your provider is compatible with your devices. Remember that some routers are incompatible with VPNs, so check yours.

2. **Ease of use and customer service**

   Most VPN software is easy to use. If you're using a VPN to secure your connection, your provider likely has extensive tutorials and resources you can use. If you prefer customer service, read a few online reviews to see how other consumers rate the provider's service.

3. **Internet connection speed**

   Your device and the VPN protocols will determine your internet connection speed. Encrypting data can use up significant processing power. Check if your processor and router can handle a VPN without slowing down.

   Tools like Speed test can measure a change in speed after you connect through a VPN.

Why do you need a VPN?

Nobody likes to be watched or followed in their footsteps, even if there is nothing to hide. Therefore, it is an excellent idea to improve your level of privacy. Your traffic is encrypted when you access the web using a VPN, making it exceptionally harder for anyone to spy on your online behavior. Your surfing history, communications, and other private information are valuable to the government, enterprises, and internet providers. And what is the best way to hide this data? Use a VPN that encrypts your traffic, hides your IP, and covers your online tracks. You can use it at home, at work, and on the go for uninterrupted protection.

Do you want to access specific content?

If you want to access content from your country while traveling the world, a VPN can help. Install VPN on your device, and you'll never miss out on your friends' social media posts again.

Do you use public Wi-Fi networks regularly?

VPNs protect your connection on public Wi-Fi networks so that you can browse in complete privacy. Despite the numerous ways hackers can steal your data through public hotspots, using a VPN makes your web traffic untraceable.

VPN VS. Proxy

A brief comparison between the two is provided below:

Proxy servers do not encrypt your traffic, whereas VPNs do. A VPN shields you from ISP tracking, governmental monitoring, and hackers. Proxy servers don't, thus never handle sensitive data with them.

While most proxies only reroute the traffic of a single program or browser because they operate at the application level, VPNs reroute all your traffic through a VPN server since they work at the operating system level.

Although VPNs, which must encrypt your sensitive data, can be slower than proxies, there are techniques to speed up your internet connection and web browsing.

VPNs are usually paid (you shouldn't trust free VPN services as they have limitations and tend to mine your data), while many proxy servers are free.

A VPN connection is more reliable, while proxy server connections drop more frequently.

> **NOTE:**
>
> A VPN *and a proxy are similar because they hide your* IP *address and redirect your traffic through a different machine. The advantages of a* VPN *over a proxy server are considerable, and you should unquestionably select a* VPN *if your security and privacy are essential.*

Using Proxy Technology for AST (Interception Proxies)

An intercept proxy is a tool that combines a proxy server (the server in this case is the application, not a physical server) with a gateway. It sits between your browser and your internet connection. Connections made by client browsers are redirected through the proxy with/without client-side configuration, allowing the transmission of the request/response to be altered, usually in a way NOT intended by the developer/protocol. This is by far the most valuable tool you will use in your web application vulnerability assessments/attacks. This completely opens up the apps for thorough inspection and manipulation.

Overview of Burp Suite

Burp Suite was developed by the company named Portswigger, which is also the alias of its founder, Dafydd Stuttard. Burp Suite aims to be an all-in-one set of tools and its capabilities can be enhanced by installing add-ons that are called Capp's.

It is the most popular tool among professional web app security researchers and bug bounty hunters. Its ease of use makes it a more suitable choice over free alternatives like OWASP ZAP. Burp Suite is available as a community edition which is free, a professional edition that costs about $450 USD, and an enterprise edition that costs around $4000/year. If you are a complete beginner in Web Application Pentest/Web App Hacking/Bug Bounty, we would recommend you to just read through without thinking too much about a term.

The tools offered by Burp Suite are:

- **Spider:**

  It is a web spider/crawler that is used to map the target web application. The objective of the mapping is to get a list of endpoints so that their functionality can be observed and potential vulnerabilities can be found. Spidering is done for a simple reason that the more endpoints you gather during your recon process, the more attack surfaces you possess during your actual testing.

- **Proxy:**

  Burp Suite contains an intercepting proxy that lets the user see and modify the contents of requests and responses while they are in transit. It also lets the user send the request/response under monitoring to another relevant tool in Burp Suite, removing the burden of copy-paste. The proxy server can be adjusted to run on a specific loop-back IP and a port. The proxy can also be configured to filter out specific types of request-response pairs.

- **Intruder:**

  It is primarily used in Appsec as a fuzzing tool. This is used to run a set of values through an input point. The values are run and the output is observed for success/failure and content length. Usually, an anomaly results in a change in the response code or content length of the response. Burp Suite allows brute-force, dictionary file, and single values for its payload position. The intruder is used for:

  - Brute-force attacks on password forms, pin forms, and other such forms.
  - The dictionary attack on password forms, fields that are suspected of being vulnerable to XSS or SQL injection.

- Testing and attacking rate limiting on the web app.

➢ **Repeater:**

Repeater lets a user send requests repeatedly with manual modifications. It is used for:

- Verifying whether the user-supplied values are being verified.
- If user-supplied values are being verified, how well is it being done?
- What values is the server expecting in an input parameter/request header?
- How does the server handle unexpected values?
- Is input sanitation being applied by the server?
- How well does the server sanitize the user-supplied inputs?
- What is the sanitation style being used by the server?
- Among all the cookies present, which one is the actual session cookie?
- How is CSRF protection being implemented and is there a way to bypass it?

➢ **Sequencer:**

The sequencer is an entropy checker that checks for the randomness of tokens generated by the web server. These tokens are generally used for authentication in sensitive operations: Cookies and anti-CSRF tokens are examples of such tokens. Ideally, these tokens must be generated in a fully random manner so that the probability of appearance of each possible character at a position is distributed uniformly. This should be achieved both bit-wise and character-wise. An entropy analyzer tests this hypothesis for being true. It works like this: Initially, it is assumed that the tokens are random. Then the tokens are tested on certain parameters for certain characteristics. A term significance level is defined as a minimum value of probability that the token will exhibit for a characteristic, such that if the token has a characteristics probability below the significance level, the hypothesis that the token is random will be rejected. This tool can be used to find out the weak tokens and enumerate their construction.

- **Decoder:**

The decoder lists the common encoding methods like URL, HTML, Base64, Hex, etc. This tool comes in handy when looking for chunks of data in values of parameters or headers. It is also used for payload construction for various vulnerability classes. It is used to uncover primary cases of IDOR and session hijacking.

- **Extender:**

Burp Suite supports external components to be integrated into the tools suite to enhance its capabilities. These external components are called BApps. These work just like browser extensions. These can be viewed, modified, installed, or uninstalled in the Extender window. Some of them are supported on the community version, but some require the paid professional version.

- **Scanner:**

The scanner is not available in the community edition.

It scans the website automatically for many common vulnerabilities and lists them with information on confidence over each finding and their complexity of exploitation. It is updated regularly to include new and less known vulnerabilities. Most of the features that are available in Burp Suite are also available in OWASP ZAP, so it really comes down to the tester's preference, budget, or allowed testing conditions.

Application Security Testing Tools

Why Do We Need Application Security Tests (ASTs)?

Application Security Testing (AST) involves:

- By utilizing different testing methods, software applications' quality and security can be increased.
- Remediating.
- Ultimately preventing weaknesses and vulnerabilities in all phases of the development process of software.

This is a proven way to help prevent cyberattacks. Application security attacks are the most common form of an external attack. Therefore, improving application security is one of the security decision-makers' top priorities and concerns.

Identifying and fixing application vulnerabilities works best when it is closer to the developer and can be integrated as part of functional testing. AST tools extend automated application security testing across the SDLC to help uncover security and quality issues that could expose security risks in your software applications. This increases collaboration in DevSecOps and provides an effective way to identify and manage security risks more confidently.

This includes application security testing techniques, penetration testing, and various testing tools. It is beneficial to learn more about the types of security vulnerabilities each testing strategy can mitigate and identify the tools to improve the processes further. Application security testing is one of the best ways to protect internet-connected assets from external threats. By detecting vulnerabilities in your application, you can patch them before an attacker uses them.

This will not only protect your website and data but also protect your customers. A hacker attacking your website could gain access to sensitive consumer information, resulting in financial ruin, identity theft, or loss of confidence in your company. In short, web application security testing is essential because it can help you avoid these attacks and keep your website safe.

AST Tools

Application security (AppSec) testing tools are designed to help identify vulnerabilities and weaknesses in software applications that could be exploited by attackers. These tools are used to test the security of applications to ensure that they are secure and can be trusted to handle sensitive data.

There are several types of AppSec testing tools, each with its own focus and strengths. Here's a brief overview of the most common types:

- **Static Application Security Testing (SAST) tools:** These tools scan the application's source code to identify potential security vulnerabilities. SAST tools analyze the code for common security issues such as SQL injection, cross-site scripting (XSS), and buffer overflows.
- **Dynamic Application Security Testing (DAST) tools:** These tools simulate attacks against the running application to identify vulnerabilities that can be

exploited by an attacker. DAST tools can discover security issues such as broken authentication and access control, injection flaws, and information disclosure.

- **Interactive Application Security Testing (IAST) tools:** These tools combine SAST and DAST techniques to provide real-time analysis of running applications. IAST tools can provide in-depth analysis of an application's code while it is running, which enables them to detect security vulnerabilities that might be missed by other types of testing.

- **Web Application Firewalls (WAFs):** These are security appliances that sit in front of web applications and analyze incoming traffic to identify and block potential security threats. WAFs can be configured to detect and block common attack patterns such as SQL injection, cross-site scripting, and file inclusion attacks.

- **Code review tools:** Code review tools are software applications used by software development teams to review code and ensure that they are of high quality, meets established coding standards, and is free from security vulnerabilities.

AppSec testing tools are an important part of any organization's security strategy. By using these tools, developers and security professionals can identify potential security issues early in the software development lifecycle and reduce the risk of a successful attack.

What Is SAST?

Static Application Security Testing (SAST) analyzes source code or compiled code to identify potential vulnerabilities or security issues. SAST can help organizations identify security flaws earlier in the software development life cycle, reducing the cost and complexity of addressing vulnerabilities later in the development process. Some popular SAST tools include Checkmarx, Fortify, and Veracode.

Benefits of SAST

The benefits of SAST are many, and they include the following:

1. **Early Detection of Security Issues:** SAST allows developers to identify security issues earlier in the development process. This is important because fixing vulnerabilities discovered after a product has been released can be difficult and costly. SAST tools scan the code for potential security issues, such as buffer overflows, SQL injection, and cross-site scripting (XSS) attacks, highlighting them to the developer.

2. **Cost-Effectiveness:** SAST is a cost-effective solution for identifying security issues in software. Compared to other security testing methods, such as manual code reviews or penetration testing, SAST is less expensive and can be used throughout the development process.

3. **Integration with CI/CD Pipelines:** SAST can be integrated with continuous integration/continuous deployment (CI/CD) pipelines, allowing developers to identify and fix security issues in real-time. This helps to reduce the time and cost of addressing vulnerabilities later in the development process.

4. **Increased Developer Productivity:** SAST tools automate identifying security issues in the code, freeing developers to focus on other tasks. This leads to increased productivity and faster time-to-market for software products.

How SAST Works

SAST analyzes the source code or compiled code for potential security issues. SAST tools use a combination of pattern matching, code analysis, and data flow analysis to identify vulnerabilities.

- **Pattern Matching:** SAST tools use pattern matching to identify security issues in the code. The tools search for specific patterns that are known to be associated with vulnerabilities, such as the use of dangerous APIs or the presence of invalidated input.

- **Code Analysis:** SAST tools perform code analysis to identify potential security issues. Code analysis involves examining the code to identify potential vulnerabilities, such as buffer overflows, SQL injection, and cross-site scripting (XSS) attacks.

- **Data Flow Analysis:** SAST tools also use data flow analysis to identify potential security issues. Data flow analysis involves examining the flow of data through the application to identify potential vulnerabilities, such as invalidated user input or the presence of sensitive data in the code.

Limitations of SAST

Despite its many benefits, SAST does have limitations that developers and security teams should be aware of.

- **False Positives:** SAST tools can produce false positives, which are security issues that are reported but do not exist. False positives can take much time to examine and make users lose hope in the technology.

- **Limited Scope:** SAST tools are limited in scope and may not identify all potential security issues in the code. For example, SAST tools may not identify problems related to the configuration of the server or issues related to the interaction between different application components.

- **Limited Effectiveness for Certain Types of Vulnerabilities:** SAST tools may not be effective at identifying certain types of vulnerabilities, such as those introduced through third-party libraries or those introduced through social engineering.

The Best Practices for SAST

- **Choose the right SAST solution:** Several SAST solutions are available in the market. Before selecting a SAST solution, consider the compatibility with your programming languages, frameworks, and application servers. Evaluate the features, including coverage, accuracy, and reporting capabilities. Choosing the right solution to support your application development cycle is essential.

- **Integrate SAST into CI/CD pipeline:** Integrating SAST into the Continuous Integration/Continuous Deployment (CI/CD) pipeline is essential for detecting vulnerabilities early in the development cycle. It ensures that the code is scanned for security vulnerabilities in every stage of the SDLC. When integrated into the CI/CD pipeline, SAST provides feedback on vulnerabilities as soon as the code is committed.

- **Customize SAST configurations:** Most SAST solutions provide the flexibility to customize the configuration. It is mission critical to configure SAST to match your application's architecture and the associated attack surface. You can set rules for specific languages and frameworks, exclude directories or files, and define custom rules for particular threats.

- **Ensure complete code coverage**: SAST should scan all the code bases, including third-party libraries and dependencies, to ensure comprehensive code coverage. Make sure to configure SAST to include all the relevant files, directories, and configurations. Partial scanning can miss critical vulnerabilities and create a false sense of security.

- **Prioritize and categorize vulnerabilities:** SAST reports can be overwhelming with a vast amount of information. Understanding the reporting format and the types of vulnerabilities detected by the tool is essential. Categorize the vulnerabilities by severity and prioritize the ones that require immediate attention. SAST reports should guide the remediation process and ensure that the vulnerabilities are adequately addressed.

- **Collaborate with development and security teams:** SAST is not a one-time activity but requires collaboration between development and security teams. SAST should be integrated into the development process, and the results should be shared with the development team. The development team can then prioritize and fix the vulnerabilities as part of the SDLC. This collaboration ensures that security is not an afterthought and is included from the beginning of the development process.

- **Monitor SAST regularly:** Regular monitoring of SAST is crucial to ensure the solution is functioning correctly. Monitor the SAST logs for errors, warnings, or other issues that may impact the results. Also, ensure the SAST solution is up-to-date with the latest patches and software updates.

SAST is an essential tool for identifying security issues in software. SAST tools allow developers to identify vulnerabilities earlier in the development process, reducing the cost and complexity of addressing security issues later in the development process. However, SAST does have limitations, including the potential for false positives and the limited scope of the tool.

What is DAST?

A security testing method, DAST, is used to find security flaws in online applications. It is a type of black-box testing performed on a running application to identify security weaknesses. Unlike static application security testing (SAST), which analyzes an application's source code, DAST examines the application as it is running. The purpose of DAST is to identify security vulnerabilities that an attacker may exploit to gain unauthorized access to sensitive data or cause harm to the application.

Benefits of DAST

DAST offers several benefits, making it a valuable technique for securing web applications. Some of these benefits include:

- **Coverage:** DAST covers a wide range of security vulnerabilities, including those that are difficult to detect using other testing techniques.
- **Accuracy:** DAST produces accurate results because it tests the application in its virtual environment.

- **Efficiency:** DAST is an efficient testing technique that can identify vulnerabilities quickly, enabling developers to fix them before attackers exploit them.

- **Automation:** DAST can be automated, reducing the need for manual testing and enabling developers to test their applications more frequently.

How DAST Works

DAST sends various HTTP requests to a web application and analyzes the responses for signs of vulnerabilities. The testing tool can be configured to simulate different attacks, such as SQL injection, cross-site scripting (XSS), and directory traversal. The agency then reports any vulnerabilities, along with recommendations for how to fix them. DAST tools typically work in the following way:

The tool is configured to scan the web application, specifying the URLs to be tested and the types of attacks to be simulated.

- The tool sends a series of requests to the application, including routine and malicious requests, and analyzes the responses for signs of vulnerabilities.

- The tool reports any vulnerabilities it finds, along with recommendations for fixing them.

- The developer fixes the vulnerabilities and re-runs the DAST tool to ensure they have been successfully addressed.

Key Concepts of DAST

Several key concepts are essential to understand when using DAST. These include:

- **Black-box testing:** DAST is a type of black-box testing because it tests the application without knowledge of its internal workings.
- **HTTP requests:** DAST sends various HTTP requests to the application and analyzes the responses.
- **Simulated attacks:** DAST tools simulate different attacks to identify vulnerabilities.
- **False positives:** DAST tools can produce false positives and report vulnerabilities that do not exist.
- **False negatives:** DAST tools can also produce false negatives, which are vulnerabilities that are not reported.

The Best Practices For DAST

It is critical to adhere to several best practices to make the most of DAST. A few of these are:

- **Use multiple DAST tools:** Different tools may identify different vulnerabilities, so it is a good idea to use more than one DAST tool.
- **Configure the tool correctly:** It is essential to configure the DAST tool correctly, specifying the URLs to be tested and the types of attacks to be simulated.

- **Address false positives:** False positives can be time-consuming to address, so it is essential to minimize them by configuring the tool correctly and filtering out known false positives.

- **Follow up on vulnerabilities:** Once vulnerabilities are identified, it is essential to follow up on them and ensure that they are correctly fixed.

Dynamic Application Security Testing (DAST) is a critical security testing technique used to identify security vulnerabilities in web applications. It offers several benefits, including comprehensive coverage, accuracy, efficiency, and automation, making it a valuable tool for securing web applications.

DAST sends various HTTP requests to a web application and analyzes the responses for signs of vulnerabilities. The testing tool can be configured to simulate different attacks, such as SQL injection, cross-site scripting (XSS), and directory traversal. The device then reports any vulnerabilities, along with recommendations for how to fix them.

To make the most of DAST, it's essential to follow a few best practices, such as employing various DAST tools, configuring the tool correctly, handling false positives, and keeping track of vulnerabilities.

DAST is critical to any comprehensive security testing program for web applications. It enables developers to identify and address security vulnerabilities before they are exploited by attackers, helping to protect sensitive data and ensure the secure and reliable operation of web applications.

Interactive Application Security Testing (IAST)

Security testing, known as IAST, or interactive application security testing, tries to find security flaws in an application as it is being used. IAST was created to assist developers and security experts in finding and quickly resolving security problems before attackers could take advantage of them.

IAST is a security testing methodology that combines both SAST (Static Application Security Testing) and DAST (Dynamic Application Security Testing) techniques. It is an automated testing approach that runs alongside the application being tested, looking for security vulnerabilities as the application is used. IAST instruments the application code, monitors its behavior, and identifies security vulnerabilities by analyzing its execution path.

How Does IAST Work?

IAST instruments the application under test by injecting sensors into the code. These sensors capture data about the application's behavior, such as input and output data, runtime variables, and control flow. IAST then analyzes this data to identify potential security vulnerabilities in the application.

The main advantage of IAST is that it can detect vulnerabilities that are difficult or impossible to find with other testing approaches. For example, IAST can identify vulnerabilities that depend on specific input values, user permissions, or other runtime conditions. IAST can also detect vulnerabilities that are introduced by third-party libraries or components.

Benefits Of IAST

- **Faster time-to-detection**: IAST can detect security vulnerabilities in real-time, allowing developers to fix them quickly and efficiently. This means that IAST can help reduce the time it takes to identify and fix vulnerabilities, which is critical for constantly evolving applications.

- **More accurate results:** Because IAST analyzes the application's behavior in real-time, it can provide more precise results than other testing approaches that rely on static or manual analysis. IAST can detect more complex vulnerabilities that different testing approaches might miss.

- **Reduced false positives:** IAST can reduce the number of false positives by analyzing the application's behavior in real-time. This means that IAST can provide more precise results, reducing the number of false alarms and allowing developers to focus on the most critical vulnerabilities.

- **Integration with development processes:** IAST can integrate with development processes, allowing developers to identify and fix vulnerabilities as part of their everyday workflow. This means that developers can fix vulnerabilities quickly and efficiently, reducing the risk of security breaches.

Limitations Of IAST

- **Performance overhead:** Because IAST instruments the application code and analyzes its behaviors in real-time, it can have a performance overhead that might affect the application's performance. This also slows code execution due to the method of analysis. IAST should be used in a controlled environment to avoid impacting the application's performance.

- **Limited coverage:** IAST can only detect vulnerabilities that occur during runtime. IAST might not detect vulnerabilities introduced during the development process, such as those presented by third-party libraries or components.

- **Limited language support:** IAST might not support all programming languages, which might not be suitable for all applications.

The Best Practices For IAST

- **Choose the right IAST solution:** Several IAST solutions are available in the market. Before selecting an IAST solution, consider the compatibility with your programming languages, frameworks, and application servers. Evaluate the features, including coverage, accuracy, and reporting capabilities. Choosing the right solution to support your application development cycle is essential.

- **Integrate IAST into CI/CD pipeline:** Integrating IAST into the Continuous Integration/Continuous Deployment (CI/CD) pipeline is essential for detecting vulnerabilities early in the development cycle. It ensures that the code is scanned for security vulnerabilities in every stage of the SDLC. When integrated into the CI/CD pipeline, IAST provides feedback on vulnerabilities as soon as the code is committed.

- **Ensure proper instrumentation:** IAST requires instrumenting your application with sensors that can capture runtime data. The sensors need to be correctly configured and installed to ensure that they capture accurate data. IAST instruments can be integrated into the code via static linking, dynamic linking, or as a loadable module. Make sure to verify that the instrumentation does not impact the performance of your application.

- **Customize IAST configurations:** Most IAST solutions provide the flexibility to customize the configuration. It is crucial to configure IAST to match your application's architecture and the associated attack surface. You can set rules for specific languages and frameworks, exclude directories or files, and define custom rules for particular threats.

- **Test in a representative environment:** Testing IAST in a familiar environment is essential. The test environment should match the production environment as closely as possible. This ensures that IAST detects all the vulnerabilities and that there are no false positives or negatives. It's recommended to test IAST in different environments, such as dev, Test, and production, to ensure the solution is suitable for all.

- **Understand the IAST reporting:** IAST reports can be overwhelming with a vast amount of information. Understanding the reporting format and the types of vulnerabilities detected by the tool is essential. Categorize the vulnerabilities by severity and prioritize the ones that require immediate attention. IAST should be used to guide the remediation process and to ensure that the vulnerabilities are adequately addressed.

- **Monitor IAST regularly:** Regular monitoring of IAST is important to ensure the solution is functioning correctly. Monitor the IAST logs for errors, warnings, or other issues that may impact the results. Also, ensure the IAST solution is up to date with the latest patches and software updates.

IAST is a powerful security testing approach that combines the benefits of SAST and DAST. It can provide faster time-to-detection, more accurate results, and reduced false positives. However, IAST has some limitations, such as performance overhead, limited coverage, and language support. Nevertheless, IAST is a valuable addition to any security testing program, providing developers with a way to identify and fix vulnerabilities quickly and efficiently.

Mobile Application Security Testing (MAST)

With the increasing popularity of mobile applications, security has become a primary concern for developers and users alike. Mobile applications often contain sensitive personal, financial, and location data, making them a prime target for attackers.

Due to their increasing importance in our everyday lives, mobile applications have become a top target for attackers attempting to take advantage of their security vulnerabilities. Mobile Application Security Testing (MAST) has become increasingly important to ensure the security of mobile applications. MAST involves identifying and mitigating vulnerabilities in mobile applications by performing security testing using specialized tools.

Types of Vulnerabilities in Mobile Applications

Several types of vulnerabilities can be found in mobile applications. Some of the most common vulnerabilities include:

- **Insecure Data Storage** - Applications that store sensitive data on the device in an unencrypted format are vulnerable to attack. Attackers can quickly access this data and use it for malicious purposes.

- **Insecure Communication** - Applications that communicate with servers over an insecure channel are vulnerable to man-in-the-middle attacks. Attackers can intercept the data being transmitted and modify it to their advantage.

- **Code Injection** - Applications that accept user input without proper validation are vulnerable to code injection attacks. Attackers can inject malicious code into the application, which can be used to steal sensitive data or take control of the device.

- **Unauthorized Access** - Applications that do not adequately authenticate users are vulnerable to unauthorized access. Attackers can gain access to sensitive data or functionality without proper authorization.

MAST Tools

MAST tools are designed to help identify and mitigate vulnerabilities in mobile applications. These tools can be used to perform various tests, including static analysis, dynamic analysis, and penetration testing.

Here are some of the most popular MAST tools available:

- **Mobile Security Framework (MobSF):** MobSF is an open-source mobile application security testing framework that can be used for Android and iOS applications. It provides a wide range of features, including static analysis, dynamic analysis, and malware analysis.

- **Appknox:** Appknox is a cloud-based mobile application security testing platform that provides both automated and manual testing capabilities. It can be used to test both Android and iOS applications and provides detailed reports on vulnerabilities found.

- **Zed Attack Proxy (ZAP)**: ZAP is a popular open-source web application testing tool that can be used to test mobile applications. It can be used to test Android and iOS applications and offers static and dynamic analysis.

Mobile applications have become integral to our daily lives, and their security is of utmost importance. MAST tools can be used to identify and mitigate vulnerabilities in mobile applications, ensuring that they are secure and safe for users to use.

Application Protections: WAF and RASP Technologies

Web Application Firewalls (WAFs)

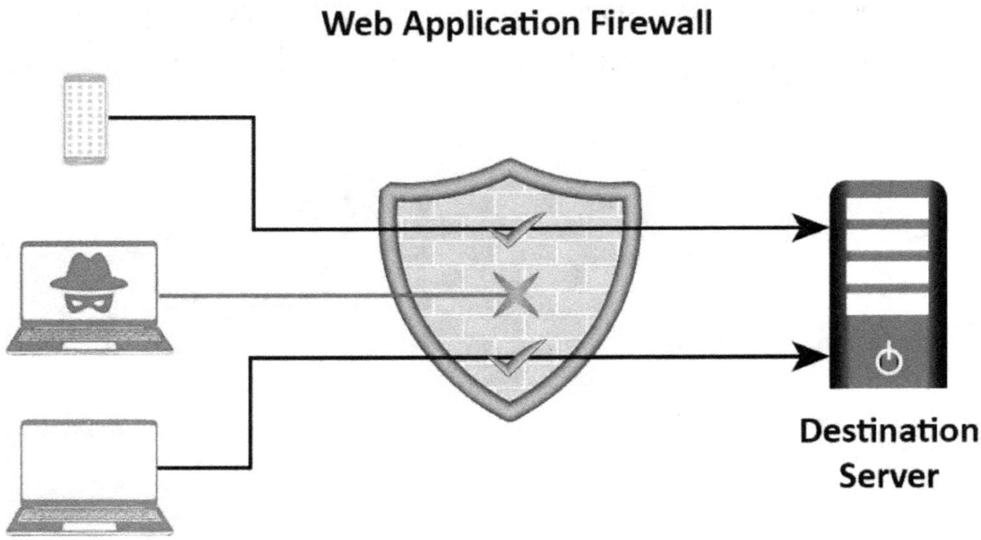

What Is a Web Application Firewall (WAF)?

Web Application Firewalls (WAFs) are security tools that protect web applications from various attacks, including SQL injection, cross-site scripting (XSS), and other application layer attacks. Data packets going to and from a website or web application are watched, filtered, and restricted by a web application firewall (WAF). A WAF is typically deployed using a reverse proxy and positioned in front of one or more websites or apps. It might be network-based, host-based, or cloud-based. The WAF inspects each packet and employs a rule base to evaluate Layer 7 web application logic and filter out potentially dangerous traffic that can aid web exploits. It can run as a network appliance, server plugin, or cloud service.

WAFs are a common security control used by enterprises to protect web systems against zero-day exploits, malware infections, impersonation, and other known and unknown threats and vulnerabilities. Through customized inspections, a WAF can detect and immediately prevent several of the most dangerous web application security flaws, which traditional network firewalls and other intrusion detection systems (IDSes) and intrusion prevention systems (IPSes) may not be capable of doing. WAFs are especially useful to companies that provide products or services over the internet, such as e-commerce shopping, online banking, and other interactions between customers or business partners.

Web applications have become an integral part of modern businesses and organizations, providing users access to a wide range of services and information over the internet. At the same time, the growth of the internet has also created new security risks and vulnerabilities that need to be addressed to ensure the safety and security of sensitive information. Firewalls play a heavy role in protecting web applications and networks by regulating incoming and outgoing traffic and preventing unauthorized access.

WAF Architecture

A WAF typically consists of two main components: a policy engine and a set of rules. The policy engine manages the WAF configuration, while the rules define how incoming web traffic should be inspected and blocked if necessary.

WAFs are often implemented as a reverse proxy, sitting between the user's browser and the web server. In this configuration, the WAF intercepts all incoming web traffic, forwarding legitimate traffic to the web server and blocking any malicious traffic. WAFs can also be deployed as a cloud service, offering protection for web applications hosted on cloud platforms.

WAFs Use a Variety of Techniques To Detect and Block Attacks

The variety of techniques to detect and block attacks or threats includes:

- **Signature-based detection:** WAFs can use signature-based detection to identify known attacks based on their unique signatures. The WAF compares incoming web traffic to a database of known attack signatures, blocking any traffic that matches.

- **Protocol anomaly detection:** WAFs can analyze web traffic for protocol anomalies, such as requests that violate the HTTP protocol. For example, if a request contains many HTTP headers, the WAF may block the proposal, as it could be an attempt to exploit a vulnerability in the web server.

- **Behavioral analysis:** WAFs can analyze web traffic for abnormal behavior, such as repeated requests for the same resource. This could indicate an attack, and the WAF may block subsequent requests from the same IP address.

- **Machine learning:** WAFs can use machine learning algorithms to identify and block attacks that have not been seen before. Machine learning algorithms can analyze web traffic in real-time, identifying patterns and anomalies that may indicate an attack.

Benefits of WAFs

WAFs offer a range of benefits to organizations, including:

- **Protection against a wide range of attacks:** WAFs can protect web applications against a wide range of attacks, including SQL injection, XSS, and other application layer attacks.
- **Easy to deploy:** WAFs are easy to deploy and can be installed as software or a cloud service.
- **Low false favorable rates:** WAFs typically have low false positive rates, meaning they do not block legitimate traffic.
- **Compliance reporting:** WAFs can generate reports to help organizations comply with various regulatory requirements, including GDPR, HIPAA, and PCI-DSS.

WAF Challenges

While WAFs offer many benefits, there are also several challenges associated with their use. These include:

- **False negatives:** WAFs can miss certain types of attacks, particularly those that are sophisticated and targeted.
- **False positives:** WAFs can generate false positives, blocking legitimate traffic and causing disruptions to web applications.
- **Complexity:** WAFs can be complex to set up and configure, requiring specialized knowledge and expertise.

- **Performance impact:** WAFs can impact web applications, particularly if they are not properly configured.

Web Application Firewalls (WAFs) are essential to any organization's web application security strategy. By providing protection against a wide range of attacks, WAFs can help organizations reduce the risk of a security breach. While challenges are associated with using WAFs, their benefits make them an essential component of any comprehensive web application security strategy.

Why Is WAF Security Important?

Many businesses that provide online goods or services, such as social media service providers, digital institutions, and developers of mobile applications, require WAFs. A WAF can safeguard sensitive information, including customer and credit card information, and stop leakage.

Corporations often store the majority of sensitive data in a backend database that is accessible through web applications. Businesses use mobile apps and IoT devices frequently to streamline business interactions, with many online transactions taking place at the application layer. For access to this data, attackers target specific software.

The PCI DSS (Payment Card Industry Data Security Standard), which applies to any organization handling cardholder data and requires the creation of a firewall, is one compliance standard that can be satisfied by implementing a WAF. The security model of an entity must therefore include a WAF.

To create a defense-in-depth security paradigm, it is advised that you integrate a WAF with additional security measures, including intrusion detection systems (IDS), network monitoring systems (IPS), and conventional firewalls.

WAF Implementation Approaches

Three methods or a hybrid of the three can be used by WAF to examine and filter the content of these HTTP requests:

1. **Whitelisting:**

   The WAF will, by default, reject all requests and only permit those known to be trusted under a whitelisting strategy. It gives a list of IP addresses that are believed to be secure. Compared to blacklisting, whitelisting requires fewer resources. The drawback of a whitelisting strategy is that it could unintentionally stop good visitors. It has the potential to be effective and throws a large net, yet it might also be inaccurate.

2. **Blacklisting:**

   A blacklisting strategy employs pre-defined signatures to prohibit harmful online traffic and guard against vulnerabilities in websites or web applications by default, allowing packets to pass. It is a collection of guidelines for identifying malicious packets. Since public websites and online applications receive a lot of traffic from anonymous IP addresses that aren t known to be malicious, blacklisting is more effective.

   A blacklisting technique has the disadvantage of using more resources; in contrast to using trusted IP addresses by default, it requires more data to filter packets based on specific attributes.

3. **Hybrid security:**

   Blacklisting and whitelisting components can be found in a hybrid security model. The most notable point is that a WAF analyzes HTTP transactions and reduces or, preferably, removes dangerous traffic before it reaches a server for processing, regardless of the security architecture it employs.

Types Of Web Application Firewalls

- **Network-based WAFs:** These are typically hardware-based and can lower latency because they are installed as near the application as possible locally on-premises via a dedicated appliance. Replication of rules and settings across various appliances is made available by the majority of the primary network-based WAF providers, allowing for extensive deployment, setup, and management. The expense of this WAF product is its most significant disadvantage because it requires both initial capital investment and continual maintenance.

- **Host-based WAFs:** These may be formed and maintained in the software's source code. A host-based WAF implementation has the advantages of being more affordable and enabling more configuration possibilities. Because they involve application libraries and rely on local server resources to function, host-based WAFs can be challenging to manage. More human resource management may be needed, including developers, system analysts, and DevOps/DevSecOps.

- **Cloud-hosted WAFs:** These provide a low-cost option for businesses looking for a fully operational product with little setup and requirements. Cloud WAFs frequently require a minor update to the domain name system (DNS) or proxy to reroute application traffic. They are also simple to set up and offered on a subscription basis. Although it can be challenging to delegate control over filtering web application traffic to a third-party provider, the approach enables applications to be protected across various hosting environments and uses similar policies to thwart application layer attacks. These third parties also have access to the most recent threat intelligence, which they can use to help recognize and counter the most recent risks to application security.

Stateless WAFS Vs Stateful WAFS

A WAF sits between a company's web applications and the requests coming in from the internet. Via reverse proxy, it monitors, filters, or blocks data packets as they travel to and from a web application. In doing so, it attempts to screen out potentially harmful traffic that may enable web exploits. A WAF may come from a cloud-based solution, an appliance, a server plugin, or a filter.

During the first generation of WAFs, **Stateless WAFs** used static rules to analyze potential threats arriving via inbound requests to a company's web application servers. Using pattern recognition, they effectively generated educated guesses on how a web application might react to a specific form of attack using predetermined models of application behavior and attack behavior. For example, Stateless WAFs might check how quickly requests were coming in, whether they originated from the same source, and other behavioral metrics that might indicate malicious activity was underway.

Stateless WAFs could perform such tasks much more rapidly than their human counterparts, but they needed to be more adaptable and nimbler enough to ward off evolving attacks successfully. A continual game of cat and mouse ensued in which attackers, upon discovering that their initial attack on a web application had been unsuccessful, would devise a new form of attack behavior that the WAF had not seen before and could not prevent. Then, when the WAF eventually received new rules that could ward off this new attack variant, the attackers would come up with yet another method for evading detection.

The second generation of WAFs, known as **Stateful WAFs,** offers more agile defenses than its predecessor. Stateful WAFs can enrich collected data with relevant context and analyze a web application's current threat landscape. Since they take a broader, more contextual view into account, Stateful WAFs are better at detecting critical issues such as DDoS attacks and "low and slow" attacks that attempt to undermine security by flying under the radar.

Advantages of Web Application Firewalls (WAF)

Because it provides better insight into sensitive application data transmitted across the HTTP application layer, a WAF has an advantage over conventional firewalls. It can stop application layer assaults like the ones listed below, which often get past standard network firewalls:

1. Attackers can insert and run malicious scripts in another user's browser, thanks to cross-site scripting (XSS) vulnerabilities.

2. Any program that uses a SQL database is susceptible to SQL injection attacks, which give hackers access and the capacity to alter sensitive data.

3. Attackers can assume the identity of a legitimate user by stealing a session ID, thanks to web session hacking. A cookie or Uniform Resource Locator stores a session ID (URL).

4. DDoS attacks overwhelm a network by saturating it with traffic to the point that it cannot serve its users. Network firewalls and WAFs can both stop this kind of assault, but they do it from different angles.

A WAF also has the benefit of being able to defend web-based applications without necessarily having access to their source code. A cloud-hosted WAF can secure the application without requiring access, in contrast to host-based WAFs that can be embedded into application code. A cloud WAF also offers quick virtual patching options that let users quickly modify their settings to newly discovered threats and is simple to set up and operate.

The Different Ways to Deploy a WAF

There are various ways to deploy a WAF. For instance, everything relies on where you deploy your applications, what services you need, how you want to maintain them, and how flexible and efficient an architecture you need. Do you wish to handle it yourself or outsource control of it? Is a cloud-based version preferable, or do you prefer that your WAF be installed on-site? What WAF is best for you will depend on how you want to deploy it. WAF deployment mode choices are as follows:

1. **Cloud-based + Fully Managed as a Service:** This is an excellent option if you require the fastest, most hassle-free way to get WAF in front of your apps (mainly if you have limited in-house security/IT resources).

2. **Self-Managed + Cloud-Based:** Take the benefit of the cloud's flexibility and portability of security policies while still having control over traffic management and security policy settings.

3. **Cloud-based + Auto-Provisioned:** This is the easiest way to get started with a WAF in the cloud, deploying security policy in an easy, cost-effective way.

4. **On-premises Advanced WAF (virtual or hardware appliance):** This meets the most demanding deployment requirements where flexibility, performance, and more advanced security concerns are mission critical.

3 Tips for Success with Deploying a WAF

Here are three tips to ensure that you successfully maximize the benefits of a WAF:

1. **Make sure your WAF supports your application security objectives**

   Many WAF solutions are available, each with varying security features and techniques for identifying and preventing attacks. Make sure that any WAF you choose supports your specific application security objectives.

2. **Carefully evaluate and test your WAF solution**

   To truly understand how a WAF can be an integral part of your application security program, it may be beneficial to test any WAF solution you are evaluating before making a final decision on whether to implement it. That way, you can assess and understand how it will function in coordination with other application security tools you may be using, such as RASP, since these technologies are not mutually exclusive and can be used in tandem for the most comprehensive coverage.

3. **Consider what in-house resources you will need**

   While evaluating a WAF solution, consider what in-house resources you need to make the most of it. You may determine that you will need to build additional skills and capabilities within the security team, or you may want to consider how implementing a WAF will change existing security processes your team has in place.

Businesses face increasingly sophisticated attacks on their web applications as malicious actors seek a payday from fraud and data theft. Ensuring proper web application security has never been more critical, but companies can make significant strides toward protecting their web applications and customer data by adopting a web application firewall. It's an essential part of a robust application security toolkit and a modern application security program.

Is a Web Application Firewall (WAF) needed?

With cyberattacks becoming increasingly more complex, businesses and organizations must put themselves in the best position to defend themselves and their clients from malicious intent. Companies involved in e-commerce, online financial services, and various other web-based products face a constant threat of fraud and data theft, which leaves them prone to compromised customer trust and possible regulatory disciplines.

Alongside a suite of tools, WAFs can add an essential extra layer of defense to an already robust application security program. Security professionals can leverage a web application firewall to monitor a possible attack-in-progress by receiving alerts for activity that violates predetermined guidelines and rules. This visibility ensures that security teams have the necessary capacity to fulfill regulatory standards while still maintaining the utmost protection for customer data.

What Is RASP?

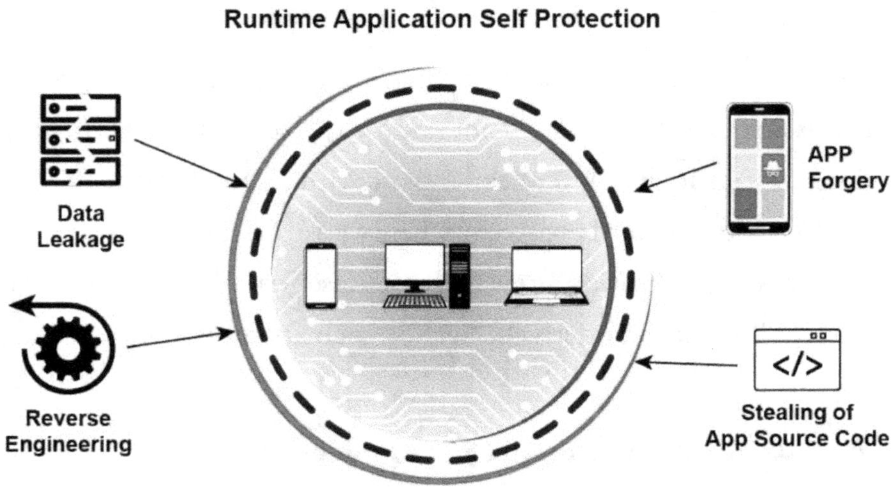

Runtime Application Self-Protection (RASP) is a security technology that enables applications to protect themselves at runtime. Traditional security tools such as firewalls, intrusion detection systems (IDS), and anti-virus software are designed to protect the network or operating system from attacks. Still, they do not cover the application itself. RASP technology is designed to provide a deeper level of protection focused on the application layer.

RASP tools work by embedding security sensors directly into the application code, which monitor the application's behaviors and detect any suspicious activity. These sensors can see many attacks, including SQL injection, cross-site scripting (XSS), buffer overflows, and more. Once an attack is detected, the RASP tool can immediately block the attack, log the incident, or alert security personnel.

RASP Tools Offer Several Advantages Over Traditional Security Tools

- **Deeper Level of Protection:** RASP tools provide a deeper level of protection than traditional security tools because they are designed to protect the application layer directly.

- **Real-Time Protection:** RASP tools can detect and respond to attacks in real-time, which is critical for protecting against fast-moving threats such as zero-day exploits.

- **Application-Specific Protection:** RASP tools are designed to protect specific applications, so they can be customized to address the unique security needs of each application.

- **Reduced False Positives:** RASP tools are embedded in the application code, so they have a better understanding of the application's behavior, which reduces false positives.

- **Integration with Development Process:** RASP tools can be integrated into the development process so that security can be built into the application from the ground up.

Different Types of RASP Tools

There are generally two types of Runtime Application Self-Protection (RASP) tools: bytecode instrumentation and binary instrumentation.

- **Bytecode Instrumentation RASP Tools:** These RASP tools modify the application's bytecode to add security sensors that monitor the application's behavior at runtime. These tools can detect various attacks, including SQL injection, cross-site scripting (XSS), and buffer overflow attacks. Some examples of bytecode instrumentation RASP tools include:

1. Contrast Security
2. Prevoty
3. Waratek

➢ **Binary Instrumentation RASP Tools:** These RASP tools modify the application's binary to add security sensors that monitor the application's behavior at runtime. These tools are generally less accurate than bytecode instrumentation RASP tools because they have a different level of visibility into the application's behavior. Still, they are usually easier to implement and have less impact on application performance. Some examples of binary instrumentation RASP tools include:

1. Guardicore
2. Sqreen
3. StackRox

RASPs in Summary

Some RASP tools may use a combination of bytecode and binary instrumentation techniques to provide a more comprehensive level of protection. Some RASP tools may be designed to work with specific programming languages or frameworks, while others are language-agnostic and can be used with many applications. Ultimately, the choice of the RASP tool will depend on the application's specific needs and the organization's overall security requirements.

RASP tools can be deployed in various ways, including as a standalone product, as part of a web application firewall (WAF), or as a plugin for an application server or web server. Some RASP tools are designed to work with specific programming languages or frameworks, while others are language-agnostic.

One potential downside of RASP tools is that they can be susceptible to attack themselves. If an attacker can compromise the RASP tool, they may be able to bypass its protection mechanisms and launch attacks against the application. This highlights the importance of selecting a secure RASP tool and following best practices for securing the RASP tool itself.

Overall, RASP technology is a promising approach to application security that provides a deeper level of protection than traditional security tools. By embedding security sensors directly into the application code, RASP tools can detect and respond to attacks in real-time, providing a critical layer of protection for today's increasingly complex and dynamic application environments.

WAF vs. RASP

RASP blocks malicious traffic without needing static rules utilizing the application itself. Rather than relying on predictions about how an application might behave in a particular scenario, RASP assesses actual application behavior to detect potentially malicious activity (for example, a call to a database, a request to open a file, or a recommendation to start a shell to execute a command) as it occurs. Neither of these technologies are solutions for identifying vulnerabilities in applications.

This can reduce false positives often seen when using a WAF, giving a security team more accurate insight into potential attacks in real-time. Since it uses the application itself, RASP can still assess its security even as the application is continually updated and further developed. RASP fits more readily into a continuous process because you can watch how the app behaves as you constantly push code changes instead of having to manipulate the static rules for WAF. WAF and RASP can complement one another, combining forces to provide a business with comprehensive and robust application security. Neither of these technologies are solutions for identifying vulnerabilities in applications.

Key Takeaways

1. Web Applications

- A web application is a software program that runs on a web server and is accessed through a web browser.
- Information is often stored in databases and other data storage systems by web apps, which are typically created using programming languages like HTML, CSS, JavaScript, and Python.
- Web applications can be used for various purposes, including e-commerce, social networking, content management, and collaboration.
- The architecture of a web application typically consists of a client side and a server side. The client side renders the user interface and processes user interactions, while the server handles data processing and information storage.

2. Firewalls

- An example of a network security system is a firewall, which monitors and controls incoming and outgoing traffic in line with predetermined security rules.
- Firewalls can be hardware-based, software-based, or a combination of both.
- Firewalls are designed to prevent unauthorized network access and protect sensitive information from being stolen or compromised.
- Firewalls use various techniques, including packet filtering, application layer inspection, and stateful inspection, to regulate network traffic and prevent threats.

3. Web Application Security

- Web application security refers to the measures and techniques used to protect web applications from malicious attacks and security threats.
- Threats to the security of web apps frequently occur in the form of SQL injection, cross-site scripting (XSS), cross-site request forgery (CSRF), and deserialization execution.
- To protect against these threats, web application developers must follow best practices for secure coding and implement measures such as input validation, error handling, and authentication and authorization controls.

4. Firewall Configuration

- Firewall configuration involves setting up rules and policies defining how traffic can enter and exit a network.
- Firewall configuration should consider the organization's specific needs and requirements, including the types of applications and services that need to be accessed and the level of security required.
- Common firewall configuration tasks include setting up access control lists (ACLs), defining security zones, and creating firewall policies that regulate traffic based on port numbers, protocols, and IP addresses.

Trends and Future Developments in WAFs

Web application firewalls (WAFs) are becoming increasingly important in securing web applications against various attacks, including cross-site scripting (XSS), SQL injection, and more. The following are some current trends and future developments in WAFs:

1. **Artificial Intelligence and Machine Learning:** WAFs are incorporating AI and ML algorithms to enhance their ability to detect and block malicious traffic in real-time.
2. **Cloud-based Deployment:** More organizations are moving towards cloud-based WAF solutions due to their scalability, ease of use, and cost-effectiveness.
3. **Integration with Other Security Tools:** WAFs are being integrated with other security tools, such as intrusion detection systems (IDSs) and intrusion prevention systems (IPSs), to provide a more comprehensive security solution.

4. **Real-time Analytics and Reporting:** WAFs incorporate real-time analytics and reporting capabilities to provide more detailed information about threats and security incidents.

5. **Support for Emerging Technologies:** WAFs support emerging technologies such as the Internet of Things (IoT) and blockchain to protect these devices and systems.

The trend in WAFs is towards increased automation and integration with other security tools to provide a more comprehensive security solution for web applications.

Continuous Research

1. Web Application Development

Consider registering in seminars or reading books on web application development to deepen your grasp of web applications. Topics to explore might include:

- Building dynamic web applications with HTML, CSS, JavaScript, and Python.
- Understanding the basics of database design and management.
- Implementing authentication and authorization controls in web applications.
- Secure coding practices and how to prevent common web application security threats.

2. Firewall Management

To deepen your knowledge of firewalls, consider taking courses or reading books that cover the following topics:

- understanding the principles of firewall design and operation
- managing firewall policies
- setting up and configuring firewalls, including creating access control lists (ACLs) and security zones

Bug Bounty Hunting Programs

Computer hacks are a popular occurrence for far too many businesses globally. In fact, according to some experts, there is always a probability that there will be a data breach, meaning potentially devastating trouble lurking for nearly one in three domestic and overseas businesses. In addition, there may be a high cost involved when cybercriminals breach corporate network systems.

The good news is that businesses in both the public and commercial sectors have another modern approach to be proactive and confront cybercrime. One of these is what is known as "bug bounty programs," a less challenging and increasingly effective strategy for locating and resolving network errors.

What's a Bug Bounty Program (BBP)?

Thanks to bug bounty programs, ethical hackers can analyze an organization's systems, apps, and data to find security flaws. This is instead financial compensation for cybercriminals who successfully find and report security flaws, bugs, and the like. Bug bounties allow businesses to use the community of ethical hackers, also known as *white hats*, who are permitted access to an organization's IT assets, to implement the tactics and actions of malicious attackers and highlight vulnerabilities that can be fixed before cybercriminals come knocking.

Here's how bug bounties work. A company first settles on a budget for its program and then establishes acceptable parameters (read: specifies the systems that ethical hackers can attempt to penetrate). While some businesses give carte blanche to white hats, others set clear boundaries and keep specific IT components off-limits so as not to interfere with operations, productivity, and profits.

Ethical hackers then go to work, infiltrating systems and searching for vulnerabilities that can lead to a security breach. Once a problem is discovered, the hackers (or hackers) submit a report notifying the company that engaged them of the vulnerabilities uncovered. They also present alternatives for remediation and deliver the details necessary for developers to replicate and otherwise validate the bug(s) found.

In terms of compensation, ethical hackers are paid sums commensurate with the severity of the vulnerabilities they detect. These amounts can range from a few thousand dollars to seven figures, depending upon the gravity of the security risk revealed and, of course, the size of the company in question.

Statistics state that companies pay more for bugs with high severity than for normal ones. Facebook has paid up to 20,000 USD for a single bug report, and Google has a collective record of paying 700,000 USD to researchers who reported vulnerabilities. Similarly, Mozilla pays up to 3,000 USD for vulnerabilities. A researcher from the UK called James Forshaw was rewarded 100,000 USD for identifying a vulnerability in Windows 8.1. In 2016, Apple also announced rewards of up to 200,000 USD to find flaws in iOS components, such as remote execution with kernel privileges or unauthorized iCloud access.

Bug Bounty Programs are not all the same. The process for claiming a bug bounty and what qualifies you to receive the payment differs from program to program. The company sets the rules for what it considers a problem worth paying for. It will also set out the proper format for reporting that issue and everything you need to know to replicate and verify it.

The amount of money a verified report is worth will also be different. Some companies are substantial, with huge budgets for security. Others are small businesses or startups that rely on bug bounty programs to compensate for their relatively small complement of permanent cybersecurity staff. In that case, the rewards could be more modest.

What skills are needed to hunt bugs?

A solid base of beliefs is necessary. Understanding how to read and code is necessary since you must hunt for methods that can be used by tools that have already been written, yet you can still report these to the organization. The more unique the process can lead to more enormous bounties. Knowledge of web applications and networking principles is necessary; you can only expect to accomplish something when you understand it. Another skill is knowing the OWASP Top 10 and how to leverage these methods.

How do you acquire the skills to find bugs?

A lot of self-education and experience-based learning will help. A beginner should start on websites like Pentester Academy, Hack the Box, and TryHackMe. You will be able to build more creative and complex techniques you learn as you experience various areas of bug hunting.

What equipment do you use?

In most cases, it is good to have virtual machines functioning on both desktop and/or laptop computers. Most testers are utilizing the Linux operating system, and the flavor is more of a personal preference. Kali, Parrot, and AthenaOS are suitable for those needing a tool-ready operating system.

The Testing Process

1. Know the rules

You need to review the entire program first. There is always a limit, and you have to keep it inside. The program is generally vulnerable to physical access, social engineering, and denial-of-service attacks of various kinds. Additionally, knowing if the program is a full or partial haven helps shield you from firms attempting to involve law enforcement. They also lay out the specific target and limit you to particular domains or addresses.

2. Information gathering

The second is gathering information, determining IP addresses for your targets, and finding out what defenses they have in place (for example, firewalls and intrusion detection/prevention systems)—sketching out ports and services to check for exploitable vulnerabilities. You would be surprised how many servers still sit with default settings and changing usernames.

3. Plan your engagement/test

The third part is planning out your attack. You can't just click a button and magically get in. It's also unlike TV or movies, where you open a page and find all this crazy information in three minutes. You have to dig into the information you have found. Are there reported vulnerabilities for a service that is running? Has that vulnerability been patched, and has your target fixed it? Make sure all your request lines look legitimate to trick their system and do more research. Research is one of the most critical parts—understanding the target and what vectors you can attempt to leverage.

4. Begin testing

The fourth part is the actual attack. Sometimes it's trying different methods in succession; other times, it's a slow process so you don't get flagged by the security countermeasures. This is where a person's level of skill truly comes into play.

5. Report the findings

Fifth, once you have found that issue, it is time for the report. Companies want a complete write-up of what you did and how you did it. Always include screenshots of anything unique, like specific lines of code or the forged request that worked. If you know how to fix the problem, you can also include that. Sometimes making their life a little easier by selecting something gets them a little extra money.

Preparing for a Bug Bounty Program: The Undeniable Value of Bug Bounty Programs

As companies and organizations like Facebook, Yahoo, Google, Yelp, Microsoft, and even the US Departments of Defense and Homeland Security know, bug bounty programs are advantageous for several reasons.

First and foremost, they can (1) identify system vulnerabilities—those that, if left unremedied, could be exploited by malicious hackers and cybercriminals—and (2) provide for necessary patches and fixes meant to render a network impenetrable. As such, a bug bounty can be an invaluable resource for companies looking to protect their IT assets and reputation and limit legal and financial exposure.

Likewise, despite the financial rewards paid to the ethical hackers who shine a light on an entity's network failures, these amounts are typically a fraction of the cost associated with remediating a cybersecurity incident at the hands of a criminal enterprise. No matter how expensive a bug bounty may be, a white hat's compensation will be exponentially cheaper than a data breach.

It gets even better. Because ethical hackers are only paid when they uncover a vulnerability, there's little financial risk in initiating a bug bounty program. For this reason, bug bounties are a perfect complement to regular penetration testing, which has limits. One of the drawbacks of penetration testing is that it's typically conducted by a single security professional—or a small team—testing a company's systems and applications. On the other hand, bug bounties are open to the universe of ethical hackers—hundreds if not thousands of individuals bringing to the table a breadth of experience and skillsets that best replicate the nefarious workings of cybercriminals.

For the good of all private and public entities and the people they serve, data and network breaches must be avoided at all costs, which is why it'd be wise for every company to create and incorporate bug bounty programs into their Incident Response Plans (IRPs). Data lifecycle management programs (DLMPs) this is to ensure data privacy and cybersecurity compliance.

It's important to understand that most state laws, including the new California Privacy Protection Act, require analyzing and investigating an organization's data privacy and cybersecurity program after a breach. So do state attorney generals and the Federal Trade Commission. Having a robust, evergreen IRP that includes a supervised bug bounty monitorship may serve to keep government enforcement bodies away. Even better, bug bounties, IRPs, and DLMPs can prevent or diminish risk, liability, penalties, and fines from regulators. No doubt about it, bug bounties, along with penetration testing, IRPs, DLMPs, and the work and insights of experienced legal counsel, can—together—go a long way toward maximizing available network protections and shielding IT assets from bad actors near and far.

Identifying and Reporting Vulnerabilities in Bug Bounty

A vulnerability report is a written record of a security issue or systemic flaws in an IT system, network architecture, application, or resource. Vulnerability reports can be a comprehensive set of findings from an overall security assessment or a specific notice of a weak point susceptible to exploitation. For instance, many tech companies, security providers, and cloud services companies have dedicated web pages where users can report such issues. Major tech brands such as Apple, Google, AWS, and others welcome users to perform security assessments or penetration testing. Some offer bug bounties to individuals who submit vulnerability reports deemed serious enough to require remediation. Likewise, security services vendors like Bugcrowd provide customized vulnerability report forms on their websites where researchers or *white hat* hackers can detail vulnerabilities, with fields for description of the issue, target resource, and technical severity, with the ability to attach screenshots or code snippets. Not all businesses have taken the time to build up a way for ethical hackers to contact them and safely alert them to potential security breaches.

There are a few areas to look at when seeking a point of contact, such as:

1. **Bug bounty program**: This is the right area to disclose any vulnerabilities found if an organization has a bug reward program. These are some elements of a bug bounty program:

- a method to securely get in touch with the relevant team
- principles of the activity
- the opportunity for a reward

However, reading and following the program's rules is essential, especially what is and is not considered *in scope*.

2. **Security.txt file:** Some firms have developed a security.txt file for security researchers, similar to the robots.txt file for web crawlers. The contact details for the appropriate point of contact within the organization will be listed in this file if one exists.

3. **Contact information:** Many companies offer a *Contact Us* form on their website or other ways for clients to get in touch with them. Doing so lets the IT or security team know that you may have found a security vulnerability and would like to speak with them. However, only share specifics if the right people receive the message.

4. **Domain registration:** A website's domain registration may include company employees' contact details, potentially including the webmaster's or web admin's email address. This could serve as a jumping-off point for locating the efficient team within the enterprise.

5. **Contact CERT:** Contacting your CERT is another method for reporting vulnerabilities if you can't find the appropriate person within an organization or

they aren't responding. Contacting vendors for vulnerability disclosure can be facilitated by organizations like US-CERT.

Reporting Vulnerabilities

Once you contact the appropriate person, you can send a full vulnerability report. Many firms will include a PGP key with their security contact information, and this should be done over an end-to-end encrypted messaging system like OpenPGP.

An error report should include as much information as possible about your discovered vulnerability. Important details include:

1. **Software that is impacted:** List the names and versions of all the programs you know or believe will be harmed by the vulnerability.

2. **Vulnerability description:** Give as much detail as possible on the vulnerability that was found, including its nature, location, and potential exploits. Please include a description of the vulnerability's potential severity and how an attacker would execute them.

3. **Exploit:** A Proof of Concept (PoC) or a demonstration of how the vulnerability can be exploited must be included, if possible. The operator can use this to verify the vulnerability report and test any recommended patches.

After generating a report, please send it to your contact using a secure channel. Ensure to only share information with the impacted vendor over a secure channel. After receiving and reviewing the report, the connection could request more details.

If a vulnerability is no longer a threat, vendors frequently permit the security researcher who identified it to publish a write-up. You can make your discovery public once you have permission to do so (and possibly have a post vetted by the firm).

Common Documentation and Testing Methods

The techniques above deal with the technical details of bug hunting. However, a suitable methodology is also needed if bug hunters are to find bugs quickly and with minimum effort and to do so consistently over time. To outline such a methodology, we must consider the constraints on the bug-hunting process, including time limitations, available security expertise, technology resources, tool availability, and legal implications.

Documentation Methods

1. **Process documentation:**

   Everyone involved in the process must understand what is being done, what is known about the target technology, and what directions they might follow during the process to find security bugs more quickly. Documentation is always key, mainly if the project involves many individuals with different expertise and experience or people working in physically separate locations.

2. **Results documentation:**

   Documenting the results and clearly stating what was left out of the process provides helpful information for future work.

Testing Methods

New ideas and methodologies are formed with one concept in mind: diversification. Relying on a single technique or person to hunt bugs is a bad idea and will produce limited results. Always use a mixture of styles and a team of two or more people.

There are several options for organizing a systematic hunt, depending on time and resources. The following are five of the most common approaches to testing:

1. Lone ranger mode (one person or more)

The most basic approach for an exhaustive security bug search is to dedicate an individual or team to the process on an ongoing basis. In this scenario, each person's sole responsibility is to find security bugs in all target technologies. With a team, each member covers all technologies independently and exchanges their findings with the other members. This process is best suited for long-term efforts; it does not consider strict time constraints or expectations for short-term results.

2. Time-constrained peer audit (two to three people)

In this approach, two or three people audit the same technology, sharing resources and tools. They might sit together at a computer, one auditing while the others watch and provide advice and fresh ideas. This methodology predates similar Extreme Programming techniques and ensures that the target technology is examined from different viewpoints and thus that fewer bugs will be overlooked. This method is advantageous when time is tight, and team members have similar skills and experience.

3. Assembly-line teamwork (two or more people)

When you have people with varying degrees of security expertise or many technologies that must be audited quickly, forming a bug-hunting team of people with specific skills is a good idea. Such a team might include the following:

- A seasoned security auditor with general knowledge of various technologies.
- A highly skilled person with in-depth, low-level knowledge of specific technologies, such as assembler for x86 or reverse engineering.
- An academic with theoretical cryptography knowledge.
- A QA analyst or software developer.

Given this team, the security auditor might do a cursory technology audit to spot possible weaknesses, then pass the technology to the person most suitable for dealing with that weakness. That person would further expand on the initial audit, identify bugs, and pass it on again. The process ends when a security bug is positively identified, and the team has proof of its existence. Meanwhile, the high-level security auditor has already moved on to the next technology and put another assembly line in motion. Although this method might miss several bugs in a specific technology, it also discovers many security bugs.

4. Tournament (teamwork)

For a more comprehensive effort, you can form several bug-hunting groups (organized as in previous examples), select a set of target technologies, and assign a subset of them to each group. You can then implement a tournament-like process, encouraging groups to find as many bugs as possible in a given period. The group that finds the most wins the tournament (and maybe a prize).

Although this is a highly efficient way to find numerous security bugs quickly, achieving well-documented and researched results requires the commitment of many people, considerable logistical effort, and strong project management during the tournament. It would be best to establish rules and procedures to score a *bug finding* in advance and ensure they are followed throughout the process.

5. Rotating teams

In this approach, several teams look at the same software in rotation. The first team does an audit, reports bugs, and gets them fixed, and then the second (and possibly a third) team does the same. After that, the first team starts over again, and the cycle is repeated until an established time limit is reached. Or, if it is an ongoing part of the software development process, the cycle is repeated indefinitely. This process guarantees that almost all bugs will be found and fixed; what one team misses, another will catch. Another advantage is that teams can audit and (if necessary) amend the previous team's bug fixes.

Trends and Development in Bug Bounty Hunting

Bug bounty hunting has become a growing trend in recent years as organizations seek to secure their systems and applications by engaging a global community of ethical hackers. Some of the future trends and developments in bug bounty hunting include:

1. **Increased Adoption:** Bug bounty programs will continue to gain wider acceptance and become more prevalent as more organizations realize the benefits of identifying and fixing vulnerabilities before malicious actors can exploit them.

2. **Greater Automation:** Automation tools will continue to evolve and become more sophisticated, making it easier for organizations to manage large-scale bug bounty programs and for hunters to identify and report vulnerabilities.

3. **Expansion to New Verticals:** Bug bounty programs will expand into new industries and sectors, such as the Internet of Things (IoT), automotive, and healthcare.

4. **Increased Competition**: The bug bounty market is becoming increasingly competitive, with more hunters entering the field and greater demand for high-quality vulnerability reports.

5. **Evolution of Rewards:** Organizations will offer more innovative and creative rewards for successful bug reports, beyond traditional monetary compensation, to incentivize and motivate hunters.

Bug bounty hunting will keep growing and diversifying, offering organizations seeking to strengthen their security posture and defend against cyberthreats and useful intelligence sources.

Conclusion

Application security has become a very important aspect of cybersecurity and has garnered significant attention in recent times. The development of applications has become an essential part of businesses and organizations, and it's best to ensure that these applications are secure. Application security refers to the protection of applications and the data they process, store, and transmit. Application security is an essential aspect of cybersecurity, as web applications have become primary targets for cybercriminals.

It's imperative for organizations to implement effective application security measures to secure their applications from attacks. This includes implementing web firewall applications, practicing secure coding, and using web proxies to enhance security.

As technology continues to evolve, it's important to stay up to date with the latest advancements in application security and to continuously monitor and update security measures to ensure that applications are secure and protected against cyberattacks.

The knowledge gained from this textbook is intended to help individuals and organizations take proactive steps to enhance the security of their applications and protect against potential cyberthreats.

Appendix

Additional Techniques and Considerations

Although bug bounty hunting can be challenging and profitable, it can also be crowded and hostile. Thinking outside the box and employing unique methods are crucial if you want to stand out and improve your chances of success. This content will examine a few unusual but well-respected suggestions for scouting and bug hunting that you might need assistance locating online.

1. Reverse engineering and code review

Reverse engineering involves analyzing and understanding a program's or system's inner workings to find vulnerabilities. This can be a complicated and drawn-out procedure, but it can reveal important details about how a program works and potential weak spots. To reverse engineer a program, you'll need to disassemble the code and examine it at a low level, using tools like a disassembler and a debugger.

Code review examines and analyzes source code to identify vulnerabilities and security weaknesses. This can be tedious and time-consuming, but it can be highly effective in finding vulnerabilities that other testing methods may miss. To perform a code review, you'll need to deeply understand the programming language and be familiar with common security pitfalls and best practices.

2. Network sniffing

Network sniffing involves intercepting and analyzing network traffic to identify vulnerabilities or security weaknesses. This technique can uncover unencrypted communication, misconfigured network devices, and unpatched systems. To perform network sniffing, you'll need to use a tool such as Wireshark, which allows you to capture and analyze network packets in real-time.

3. Application sandboxing

Application sandboxing involves creating a controlled environment to safely test and analyze a program or system. This can be useful for identifying vulnerabilities that may not be apparent under normal operating conditions. To create a sandbox, you'll need to use a tool such as VirtualBox or VMware, which allows you to create a virtual machine that can be used to isolate the program or system under test.

4. Collaboration

Collaboration is an often overlooked but extremely important aspect of bug hunting. By working with other experts and sharing knowledge and techniques, you can significantly improve your chances of finding and fixing vulnerabilities. To collaborate effectively, you'll need to be open to new ideas and willing to share your expertise with others.

5. Utilizing browser extensions for reconnaissance

Browser extensions can be a valuable tool for reconnaissance during bug hunting. One such extension is *Wappalyzer*, which identifies the technologies used on a website, such as content management systems and e-commerce platforms.

Another extension, *BuiltWith*, provides similar information but includes data on web frameworks and analytics tools. These extensions can help you quickly identify potential vulnerabilities and attack vectors on a target website.

6. **Creating a custom wordlist for subdomain enumeration**

   Subdomain enumeration is essential in surveillance, but relying on commonly used wordlists can lead to missed opportunities. Creating a custom wordlist that includes industry-specific terms, acronyms, and abbreviations can help you identify specific subdomains to your target. Additionally, using permutations and variations of common subdomain names can help increase the effectiveness of your enumeration efforts.

7. **Leveraging historical data to identify vulnerabilities**

   Many websites and applications have existed for years and often have a history of vulnerabilities that have been identified and fixed. Leveraging historical data to identify these vulnerabilities can help you find new attack vectors and identify potential weaknesses in the current version of the application. This can be done by researching previous bug bounty reports and penetration testing reports or by using a tool such as Archive.org to view historical snapshots of a website.

8. **Using public data breaches to gather sensitive information**

   Data breaches are unfortunately a common occurrence and can provide a wealth of information for a bug hunter. Using tools such as *Have I Been Pwned*, you can search for email addresses and usernames associated with a target organization and potentially gain access to sensitive information such as passwords and security questions. This information can be used to conduct targeted phishing or social engineering attacks.

9. Combining threat intelligence and bug hunting

Bug hunting and threat intelligence are two distinct fields, but they can be used to improve an organization's overall security. By combining the knowledge gained from threat intelligence with the techniques used in bug hunting, you can identify potential vulnerabilities before attackers exploit them. This can be done using a tool such as *Recorded Future*, which analyzes data from various sources to identify potential threats and vulnerabilities.

Utilizing these unconventional techniques can improve your reconnaissance efforts and increase your chances of finding critical vulnerabilities. Bug bounty hunting is constantly evolving, and staying on top of the latest techniques and tools is vital to success. While these are unconventional ideas not commonly found on the web, it's essential to always stay within the program's terms of service and the law and always act ethically.

By mastering these advanced bug-hunting techniques, you'll be well on your way to becoming an expert in the field. Whether working in a corporate security team or conducting independent research, these techniques will help you find and fix vulnerabilities more effectively and efficiently.

10. Source code audit

Bug hunters value source code, the foundation for a software program or device firmware, and regular communication with the team responsible for the code's creation and upkeep.

Teams of bug hunters painstakingly study the entire source code to conduct an audit, identifying and documenting each bug they find. Discovering and examining well-known improper programming techniques within the principle is the first and most efficient strategy.

The following (and frequently ignored) step involves bug hunters rereading the source code to comprehend its architecture and goals, which aids them in detecting security bugs inherent in design and implementation.

The source code audit technique, often known as RTFS (read the fine source), is suitable for experienced bug-hunting teams but does not necessitate an in-depth understanding of the underlying technologies.

Source code auditing can become agonizingly time-consuming and an energy pitfall as the amount of code or the complexity of the project rises. Selecting and auditing a representative code set, such as the code base of the software's core elements or important core modules, is a workable shortcut. Additionally, the process can be sped up and almost always results in the best outcomes when the development team offers assistance and responds to inquiries about design and implementation.

11. Black-box security testing

Sometimes, bug hunters cannot access the target technology for reverse engineering because they need to be made aware of how it functions. This might apply to firmware contained in the software, network equipment, or tamper-proof devices. In this case, bug hunters can approach the target technology as a *black box*, a unit that accepts particular inputs and generates specific outputs. They are aware of the device's function but not its mechanism.

But even a black box has a defined context, such as an operating system, computer network, or precise location, and cannot function in a vacuum. Bug hunters can examine the outputs and assess whether the black box is running securely that is, or if it is only doing the stated function and nothing else by changing various inputs or environmental factors.

For example, say our bug hunters have a web server as a black box. They'd first send it specific inputs (URL requests) and obtain certain outputs (web pages). Next, they'd send malformed requests or alter the server program's network or OS. Under typical functioning circumstances, the web server's outputs should match what is anticipated; if not, the server probably has a flaw. After that, the bug hunters would decide if it was a security flaw.

The secret is to change the surroundings and inputs to uncover security flaws, which typically stem from poor design and implementation techniques. Here, bug hunters' skills and practical experience are put to use by looking for known security bugs, such as buffer overflows, format string bugs, race conditions, cross-site scripting bugs, authorization and authentication flaws, and denial of service bugs.

Black box analysis typically requires considerable experience and time from the bug-hunting team, though it does not usually require excellent technical skills. An exception to this is when the target technology is a very specialized device that performs an obscure task.

12. Brute force

Automated tools offer a variation on the black-box testing approach. The idea here is to automatically try every possible bug-exposing input to the target program. This requires less expertise and relies on good testing tools. However, it might need to include fundamental design flaws or semantic attacks (bugs related to the inputs' meaning rather than the inputs themselves). Also, bug hunters might end up with innocuous bugs—security flaws present in the technology but unimportant in standard use.

13. Top-down analysis

The top-down analysis starts with a high-level overview of the target technology and drills down to detail once the team suspects specific weaknesses. With this approach, bug hunters first gather and analyze documentation and all available design materials for the target technology and related technologies. This might include design specifications, protocol specifications, white papers, formal descriptions of underlying cryptosystems, or Requests for Comments issued by the Internet Engineering Task Force.

From such documentation, bug hunters identify theoretical problems in the target technology's design and known issues in its related technologies. They then look at the technology in more detail to confirm or deny the existence of the theoretical bugs.

This approach requires experience in the information security field, a high-level understanding of many technologies, and a more academic approach to their problems. Its advantage is that it yields results quickly; however, it can lead to many dead ends and identify theoretical flaws that don't exist in the real world.

14. Information gathering

Finally, the quick and lazy—but often highly rewarding—approach is to search for bug reports or symptoms on all possible sources, including internet search engines, user mailing lists, newsgroups, product documentation and release notes, and product-support knowledge bases. Doing so gives bug hunters hints and sometimes specific information about possible security bugs; they can then attempt to verify their existence in the target technology.

For example, a web search for *product X* and, say, *SIGSEGV* indicates an abnormal program termination in a Unix OS and is symptomatic of certain security bugs, such as buffer overflows or formatting string bugs—will yield hundreds of results. The bug hunter can then refine the search for specific security-related terms. Next, the hunter might reproduce the bug or research the reported problems to verify their validity.

This method provides quick results and requires no great expertise or experience in security. However, the approach is not a good long-term strategy; it is unsystematic and can often lead the bug hunter on blind searches for security bugs without guaranteeing timely success.

Notable Guides and Frameworks

OWASP Testing Guide: The OWASP Testing Guide is a comprehensive resource that provides a detailed methodology for testing web applications for security vulnerabilities. It covers all major types of testing, including penetration testing, code review, and security testing.

OWASP Top 10: The OWASP Top 10 is a list of the most critical web application security risks, as identified by the OWASP organization. It provides guidance on the types of vulnerabilities to look for and how to test for them.

OSSTMM (Open-Source Security Testing Methodology Manual): The OSSTMM is an open-source methodology for performing security testing. It provides a detailed methodology for performing penetration testing, vulnerability scanning, and other types of testing.

NIST (National Institute of Standards and Technology) Cybersecurity Framework: The NIST Cybersecurity Framework is a set of best practices and guidelines for securing information systems. It can be used as a guide for performing application security testing and identifying vulnerabilities.

Bugcrowd's Vulnerability Rating Taxonomy (VRT): Bugcrowd's VRT is a system for classifying and prioritizing vulnerabilities found in bug bounty programs, it provides a standardized method for evaluating the severity of a vulnerability.

Common Compliance and Regulations to Consider:

PCI DSS (Payment Card Industry Data Security Standard): This standard requires organizations that handle credit card transactions to implement security measures, including web application security, to protect cardholder data.

HIPAA (Health Insurance Portability and Accountability Act): This regulation requires healthcare organizations to implement security measures, including application security, to protect patient health information.

GDPR (General Data Protection Regulation): This regulation requires organizations to protect the personal data of individuals in the European Union, including through application security measures.

SOX (Sarbanes-Oxley Act): This law requires public companies to implement controls, to protect financial data.

FISMA (Federal Information Security Management Act): This act requires US federal agencies to implement information security measures, to protect government information.

NIST (National Institute of Standards and Technology): This organization provides guidelines and standards for information security.

ISO/IEC 27001: This is an international standard that outlines best practices for information security management.

> **NOTE:**
>
> *It is important for organizations to understand and comply with relevant compliance and regulation requirements to ensure the security and protection of sensitive data and to avoid potential legal and financial consequences.*

Frequently Asked Questions (FAQs)

- **What is input validation and why is it important for application security?**

  Input validation is the process of checking and verifying user input to ensure it meets the requirements of the application. Input validation is important for web application security because it helps prevent attacks, such as SQL injection and XSS.

- **What is encryption and how does it help with application security?**

  Encryption is the process of converting plain text into a ciphertext that cannot be easily understood. Encryption helps with web application security by protecting sensitive information, such as passwords, from being intercepted and read by attackers.

- **What is a secure socket layer (SSL) and why is it important for application security?**

  A secure socket layer (SSL) is a protocol for establishing secure links between networked computers. SSL is important for web application security because it provides encryption for data in transit, protecting against eavesdropping and tampering.

- **What is a secure hypertext transfer protocol (HTTPS)?**

  HTTPS is a secure version of the hypertext transfer protocol (HTTP) used for transmitting sensitive information over the internet. HTTPS uses SSL or TLS to encrypt communication, ensuring that the data cannot be intercepted or tampered with.

- **What is two-factor authentication and how does it improve application security?**

  Two-factor authentication (2FA) is a method of authentication that requires a user to provide two forms of identification, such as a password and a security token. 2FA improves application security by adding an extra layer of security, making it more difficult for attackers to access sensitive information.

- **How to get started with bug bounty hunting?**

  Getting started with bug bounty hunting requires researching target companies, familiarizing yourself with the types of vulnerabilities, and practicing ethical hacking techniques.

- **Is bug bounty hunting legal?**

  Yes, bug bounty hunting is legal as long as it is done within the guidelines set by the company offering the rewards and with the proper authorization.

- **How much can a bug bounty hunter earn?**

  The amount a bug bounty hunter can earn depends on several factors, such as the severity of the vulnerability, the demand for such vulnerabilities, and the reputation of the hunter. Earnings can range from a few hundred dollars to tens of thousands of dollars.

- **How to find targets for bug bounty hunting?**

  Bug bounty hunters can find targets by researching companies that offer bug bounty programs, using platforms such as HackerOne or Bugcrowd, or keeping an eye on industry news and announcements.

- **Can you make a living from bounty hunting?**

Yes, you can make a living doing this. At first, you may attempt small bounties that pay out $100 or $200, but as you become more experienced, you can start bringing in much more significant amounts. People can find tips and make over $50,000 for it, though this is rare. You can make a good bit if you constantly find more complex bugs. The biggest catch is you have to be the first to see it, and if someone beats you to it, you don't get paid.

- **Any advice for bug bounties hunting beginners?**

Practice, like most things if you want to get good at it. Tons of resources provide you with targets to practice. Don't be discouraged if you don't find something. It is okay to fail; happens all the time. Get good at researching, discover sites, bookmark them, and keep cheat sheets of everyday things you use and understand that things change. Hacking is a big business right now, and attack methods are changing; sometimes, they change one day and then again three days later, leading us back to doing the research.

- **How to determine the severity of a vulnerability?**

The severity of a vulnerability is determined by factors such as the potential impact on the target system, the likelihood of exploitation, and the difficulty of fixing the issue.

- **What is a Zero-Day vulnerability?**

A Zero-Day vulnerability was a previously unknown security vulnerability that's being actively exploited by attackers.

- **What is the difference between a vulnerability and an exploit?**

  A vulnerability is a weakness in a software that can be exploited by an attacker, while an exploit is the actual code or technique used to take advantage of the vulnerability.

- **What is Responsible Disclosure?**

  Responsible Disclosure is the practice of responsibly reporting security vulnerabilities to the affected party, allowing them time to fix the issue before it becomes publicly known.

- **What are the most common mistakes made by bug bounty hunters?**

  The most common mistakes made by bug bounty hunters include not properly researching the target, not fully understanding the scope of the program, and not properly documenting and reporting vulnerabilities.

- **What are the benefits of using a web proxy and is it safe?**

  The benefits of using a web proxy include improved security, anonymity, and bypassing internet filters or restrictions. The safety of using a web proxy depends on the proxy's security measures, such as encryption and the use of secure protocols. It is important to use a reputable and secure proxy.

- **What is a reverse proxy?**

  A reverse proxy is a server that receives client requests and forwards them to one or more servers, returning the servers' responses back to the clients. Reverse proxies are often used for load balancing, security, and encryption.

- **What is a caching proxy?**

  A caching proxy is a proxy server that stores commonly requested web content in its cache, allowing it to quickly retrieve the content and reduce internet traffic.

- **What is a transparent proxy?**

  A transparent proxy is a proxy server that forwards client requests without modifying the request or response. The client is unaware that it is communicating with a proxy server.

- **What is a proxy chain?**

  A proxy chain is a series of proxy servers that a client's internet traffic is routed through, with each proxy server forwarding the request to the next. This allows for multiple levels of security, filtering, and anonymity.

- **What is a SOCKS proxy?**

  A SOCKS proxy is a proxy server that provides support for the SOCKS protocol, allowing for the routing of any type of internet traffic, including TCP, UDP, and ICMP.

More Tools for App Testing

Even though Burp Suite is the go-to tool for security researchers, there are other tools for testing applications in the same way that Burp Suite does. Here are some alternate tools for testing that are used in application security areas:

1. **Invicti:** This is a cloud-based security testing tool that offers a fast and efficient way to perform security assessments. It provides real-time feedback on security issues, making it easier to identify and resolve potential threats.

   Merits:

- ➢ offers comprehensive security testing for applications
- ➢ comes with an easy-to-use interface
- ➢ supports multiple platforms

2. **Acunetix**: This is a leading security testing tool that provides a comprehensive set of features to perform security assessments. It is known for its advanced web vulnerability scanner and reporting capabilities.

   Merits:

- ➢ comprehensive vulnerability scanning
- ➢ offers automatic scanning and reporting
- ➢ good user interface

3. **Intruder.io:** This is a cloud-based security testing tool that provides a fast and efficient way to perform security assessments.

Merits:

- automated security testing for applications
- good user interface
- offers an API for integration with other tools

4. **Veracode:** This is a leading security testing tool that provides a comprehensive set of features to perform software security assessments. It is known for its advanced static and dynamic analysis capabilities.

Merits:

- comprehensive security testing for various software
- offers both static and dynamic analysis
- good reporting and visualization capabilities

5. **Checkmarx:** This too can perform code analysis and security assessments. It is known for its advanced code analysis capabilities and reporting features.

Merits:

- static code analysis for security vulnerabilities
- integrates with development processes
- good reporting and visualization capabilities

6. **Rapid7:** This tool has features to perform various security assessments, including network and security assessments.

Merits:

- offers comprehensive security testing and management solutions
- good user interface
- connects to a variety of additional programs and services

7. **Synopsys:** This tool provides a comprehensive set of features to perform software security assessments. It is known for its advanced static and dynamic analysis capabilities.

   Merits:

- comprehensive security testing and management solutions
- good user interface
- connects to a variety of additional programs and services

8. **FFUF (Fuzz Faster U Fool)**: This is an open-source fuzzing tool used to discover vulnerabilities in web applications. It sends many HTTP requests to the target application and analyzes the responses. It supports various request methods, including GET, POST, and others, and can detect vulnerabilities such as SQL injections, cross-site scripting (XSS), and directory traversal.

   Merits:

- fast, flexible, and can quickly scan many URLs
- customizable options allow for fine-tuning of security tests

9. **Wfuzz**: This is a security tool used to find vulnerabilities in web applications. It is similar to FFUF in sending large requests to the target application. Still, it can manipulate and customize the recommendations, making it a more sophisticated

tool. Wfuzz supports various types of request methods and can be used to find vulnerabilities such as SQL injections, cross-site scripting (XSS), and directory traversal.

Merits:

- advanced features such as payload generation and support for HTTP methods other than GET
- customizable options for fine-tuning security tests
- open-source, making it accessible to security testers with limited budgets

10. **Wapiti:** This is an open-source security scanner that is used to find vulnerabilities in web applications. The tool is designed to be easy to use and can identify a wide range of vulnerabilities, including SQL injections, cross-site scripting (XSS), and others. Wapiti also supports various types of request methods and has a large number of plugins available to extend its capabilities.

Merits:

- support a wide range of vulnerability types, including SQL injection and cross-site scripting (XSS)
- customizable options allow for fine-tuning of security tests

Glossary

Key Terms for Application Security Operations

- **Access Control:** A security mechanism that regulates who or what can access a system or a resource.
- **Authentication:** The process of verifying the identity of a user or a system.
- **Authorization:** The process of granting or denying access to a system or a resource based on the user's identity and role.
- **Blackbox Testing:** A type of security testing that simulates an attacker's perspective, without access to the internal structure or source code of the system being tested.
- **Botnet:** A network of compromised computers controlled by a single entity, often used to launch distributed denial-of-service (DDoS) attacks or to distribute malware.
- **Bug Bounty:** A program offered by companies or organizations that rewards individuals for finding and reporting vulnerabilities in their systems or applications.
- **Application program interface security (API):** This is an overarching term referring to practices and products that prevent malicious attack or misuse.
- **Cipher:** An algorithm that encrypts or decrypts data used to secure communication or storage.

- **Command Injection:** An attack that injects malicious commands into a system, exploiting a vulnerability in input validation or execution.
- **Cross-Site Scripting (XSS):** A type of injection attack that injects malicious code into a web page viewed by other users, exploiting a vulnerability in input validation or output handling.
- **Cross-Site Request Forgery (CSRF):** A type of attack that tricks a user into performing unintended actions on an application, exploiting a vulnerability in session management or access control.
- **Cryptography:** The science of secure communication and data protection using techniques such as encryption, digital signatures, and key management.
- **Denial-of-Service (DoS):** An attack that aims to disrupt or disable the availability of a system or a resource by overwhelming it with traffic or requests.
- **Encryption:** The process of converting plaintext into ciphertext using a secret key or a public key to protect the confidentiality and integrity of data.
- **Ethical Hacking:** The practice of using the same techniques and tools as malicious hackers but with the aim of identifying and reporting vulnerabilities in a legal and responsible manner.
- **File Inclusion:** A type of vulnerability that allows an attacker to include and execute arbitrary files on a server, exploiting a flaw in the handling of file paths or input parameters.
- **Firewall:** A security device or software that controls access to a network or a system, based on predefined rules and policies.

- **Fuzzing:** A technique that involves sending random or malformed input to a system to identify unexpected behavior or crashes.
- **Hashing:** The process of converting an input into a fixed-size output using a mathematical function for the purpose of secure comparison, indexing, or integrity checking.
- **Injection:** A type of attack that injects malicious code or data into a system, exploiting a vulnerability in input validation or execution.
- **Intrusion Detection:** The process of identifying and responding to unauthorized access, misuse, or attack on a system or a network.
- **Intrusion Prevention:** The process of blocking or mitigating unauthorized access, misuse, or attack on a system or a network using techniques such as firewalls, intrusion detection systems, and security policies.
- **Key:** A value or a password used in encryption and decryption, or authentication and authorization.
- **Key Management:** The process of creating, storing, distributing, and revoking keys to ensure the security and availability of keys for encryption, decryption, authentication, and authorization.
- **Malware:** Software specifically designed to cause harm or damage to a computer or a network, such as viruses, worms, and Trojan horses.
- **Man-in-the-Middle (MitM) Attack:** A type of attack in which an attacker intercepts and modifies the communication between two parties without their knowledge or consent.

- **Network Security:** The protection of a computer or a communication network from unauthorized access, misuse, or attack.

- **Open-Source Intelligence (OSINT):** The collection, analysis, and dissemination of information from publicly available sources for the purpose of intelligence, investigation, or security.

- **Packet Sniffing:** The process of capturing and analyzing network traffic for the purpose of monitoring, troubleshooting, or security.

- **Penetration Testing:** A type of security testing that simulates an attacker's perspective, with the aim of identifying and exploiting vulnerabilities in a system or an application.

- **Phishing:** A type of social engineering attack that uses email, instant messaging, or social media to trick a user into revealing sensitive information or visiting a malicious website.

- **Public Key:** A key that is publicly available and used in public key cryptography, such as encryption, decryption, digital signature, and key exchange.

- **Public Key Infrastructure (PKI):** The system of creating, managing, distributing, and revoking digital certificates and public keys to ensure the authenticity, integrity, and non-repudiation of electronic transactions.

- **Rootkit:** A type of malware that hides its presence and its activities on a system by modifying or disguising system files, registry keys, or network packets.

- **Sandbox:** A security mechanism that isolates a process or a resource from the rest of the system to limit its access, privilege, or functionality. Security Information and Event Management (SIEM): The collection, correlation, analysis, and response to security-related data from various sources, such as network devices, servers, applications, and users.

- **Security Information and Event Management (SIEM):** The collection, correlation, analysis, and response to security-related data from various sources, such as network devices, servers, applications, and users.
- **Security Operations Center (SOC):** A centralized team or facility responsible for monitoring, analyzing, and responding to security incidents and threats.
- **Security Policy:** A set of rules and procedures that govern the security of a system or an organization, covering issues such as access control, incident response, and compliance.
- **Social Engineering:** The use of psychological manipulation or deception to trick individuals into revealing sensitive information or performing actions that compromise security.
- **Software Composition Analysis (SCA):** The process of identifying and managing open source components and libraries used in software development.
- **Spoofing:** The act of disguising oneself as another entity to gain access or trust, or to launch attacks.
- **SQL Injection:** A type of injection attack that injects malicious SQL code into a database, exploiting a vulnerability in input validation or query execution.
- **SSL/TLS:** A protocol for secure communication over the internet, using encryption, authentication, and integrity checking via public key certificates.

- **Tokenization:** The process of replacing sensitive data with a non-sensitive value or token to protect the confidentiality and integrity of the data.

- **Two-Factor Authentication (2FA):** A method of authentication that requires the user to present two forms of identification, such as a password and a fingerprint, a token, or a biometric.

- **Vulnerability:** A weakness or a flaw in a system or an application that can be exploited by an attacker to gain unauthorized access, cause damage, or steal information.

- **Vulnerability Assessment:** The process of identifying and evaluating vulnerabilities in a system or an application to prioritize and mitigate them.

- **Vulnerability Management:** The process of identifying, assessing, mitigating, and monitoring vulnerabilities in a system or an application to maintain and improve security.

- **Web Application Firewall (WAF):** A security device or software that monitors and filters incoming HTTP/HTTPS traffic to detect and prevent web application attacks.

- **Whitebox Testing**: A type of security testing that simulates an attacker's perspective, with access to the internal structure or source code of the system being tested.

- **Whitelisting:** A security mechanism that allows access or execution only for specific, trusted, or approved items, such as files, applications, or domains.

Zero-Day: A vulnerability that is unknown or unpatched, and that can be exploited by an attacker to gain unauthorized access or launch attacks before the vendor or the user is aware of it.

References

Penetration Testing Cost - Affordable Penetration Testing Pricing 2021. https://www.trustnetinc.com/penetration-testing/

MongoDB Data | Codecademy. https://www.codecademy.com/article/introduction-to-mongo-db-data

Raj, Minakshi, et al. "Do People Have an Ethical Obligation to Share Their Health Information? Comparing Narratives of Altruism and Health Information Sharing in a Nationally Representative Sample." PLoSQ One, vol. 15, no. 12, Public Library of Science, Dec. 2020, p. e0244767.

Google Hacking:What is a Google Hack? - Acunetix. https://www.acunetix.com/websitesecurity/google-hacking/

What is SIEM? | Microsoft Security. https://www.microsoft.com/en-us/security/business/security-101/what-is-siem

Maximizing IT Security: Why Vijilan SIEM is the Solution Your .... https://vijilan.com/blog/vijilan-siem-technology/

The Rise of Artificial Intelligence in Cyber Security. https://bitm.co.za/blog/-the-rise-of-artificial-intelligence-in-cyber-security

Pen Testing as A Service (PTaaS): What It Is And What It Should Do - Forbes. https://www.forbes.com/sites/forbestechcouncil/2021/05/13/pen-testing-as-a-service-ptaas-what-it-is-and-what-it-should-do/

Types of Penetration Testing: What Is, Stages - EffectiveSoft. https://www.effectivesoft.com/blog/types-of-penetration-testing.html

What Is the Best Way To Obtain SOC 2 Compliance? https://www.planetcompliance.com/what-is-best-obtain-soc-2-compliance/

Incident Response Plans in Cybersecurity. https://metaorangedigital.com/blog/incident-response-plan-in-cybersecurity/

Top 5 Most Impactful Data Breaches in IT History: Understanding. https://threws.com/top-5-data-breaches-it-history/

Cyber Security - Technology Through My Lense. https://technolense.com/cyber-security/

VMware. "What Is Application Security? | VMware Glossary." VMware, 17 Dec. 2021, https://www.vmware.com/topics/glossary/content/application-security.html

MKTG1, SISA. "10 Types of Security Testing Techniques | SISA Insights." SISA, 19 Jan. 2022,

www.sisainfosec.com/blogs/10-types-of-security-testing-techniques/. Accessed 27 Jan. 2023.

https://www.sisainfosec.com/blogs/5-most-common-application-vulnerabilities-and-how-to-mitigate-them/

Specialists, SISA-Payment Security. "5 Most Common Application Vulnerabilities and How to Mitigate Them." *SISA Information Security*, 15 Apr. 2021, www.sisainfosec.com/blogs/5-most-common-application-vulnerabilities-and-how-to-mitigate-them/..

"Reporting a Bug." *Bugcrowd Docs*, 26 Jan. 2023, https://docs.bugcrowd.com/researchers/reporting-managing-submissions/reporting-a-bug/. Accessed 28 Jan. 2023.

Protheroe, Darren, and Darren Protheroe. "Make Money with Bug Bounty Hunting Programs in 2022." *Official Darren Protheroe Finance Blog*, 29 Oct. 2022, https://darrenprotheroe.com/make-money-with-bug-bounty-hunting-programs/. Accessed 28 Jan. 2023.

Arif. "What Is Bug Bounty Hunt? What Does a Bug Bounty Hunter Do? -." *Bugbounter EN*, 22 Feb. 2022, bugbounter.com/blog/2022/02/22/what-is-bug-bounty-hunt/.

"Bug Bounty Software - PortSwigger." *Portswigger.net*, https://portswigger.net/solutions/bug-bounty-hunting.

"VPN vs. Proxy Server: What's the Difference, and Which Should You Be Using?" *Www.kaspersky.com*, 6 May 2022, www.kaspersky.com/resource-center/preemptive-safety/vpn-vs-proxy-server.

https://blog.intigriti.com/2022/05/04/how-prepare-launching-a-bug-bounty-program/

"Free Web Proxy | Anonymous Online Browsing | Hide My Ass!" *Hidemyass.com*, Hide My Ass, 2019, www.hidemyass.com/proxy. Accessed 8 Jan. 2020.

Kaspersky. "What Is a VPN and How Does It Work?" *Www.kaspersky.com*, 3 Nov. 2020, www.kaspersky.com/resource-center/definitions/what-is-a-vpn.

"FullStack.Cafe - Kill Your Next Tech & Coding Interview." *Www.fullstack.cafe*, www.fullstack.cafe/interview-questions/web-security.

What is an Application Programming Interface (API)? | IBM. https://www.ibm.com/topics/api

What Is an API–And How Are They Used? | Entrepreneur. https://www.entrepreneur.com/science-technology/what-is-an-apiand-how-are-they-used/443670

How Managed IT Services Can Benefit Your Business. https://www.itsnyc.com/2023/02/16/managed-it-services-benefit-business/

Spring WebFlux WebSocket | Vinsguru. https://www.vinsguru.com/spring-webflux-websocket/

Solenoid Valve - Detailed Introduction - U.S. Solid. https://ussolid.com/blog/solenoid-valve-detailed-introduction/

The Priceless Value of Freedom: How Decentralized Systems like the Pi https://pinetworkuniverse.blogspot.com/2023/02/the-priceless-value-of-freedom-how.html

Online application development with PowerAPPS from Microsoft .... https://melbourneonline.com.au/application-development-microsoft-power-apps/

Cloud Automation - Sigzen Technologies Pvt. Ltd.. https://www.sigzen.com/services/cloud-solutions/cloud-automation/

Ramtohul, Avinash, and Bukola Ogunleye. "REST and BPEL for E-Government Shared Services." European Conference on Digital Government, Academic Conferences International Limited, June 2017, p. 339.

API Security: Best Practices for Protecting Your Data. https://adamsechwa.hashnode.dev/api-security-best-practices-for-protecting-your-data

Physical activity – choosing the one for you - Better Health Channel. https://www.betterhealth.vic.gov.au/health/healthyliving/physical-activity-choosing-the-one-for-you

Sql Injection Prevention System - Nevon Projects. https://nevonprojects.com/sql-injection-prevention/

Recycled Plastics Market Growing Trends and Technology Forecast to 2032. https://www.linkedin.com/pulse/recycled-plastics-market-growing-trends-technology-forecast-gade

Rizwan P on LinkedIn: #testing #qa #qa #softwaretesting #development # .... https://bm.linkedin.com/posts/rizwan-p_testing-qa-qa-activity-7028950972102049792-YaUT

How to Work with Postman Environment Variables - Dotcom-Monitor. https://www.dotcom-monitor.com/wiki/knowledge-base/how-to-work-with-postman-environment-variables-in-dotcom-monitor/

Ruby on Rails Tutorial: Learn Web Development with Rails. https://www.buecher.de/shop/ruby/ruby-on-rails-tutorial-learn-web-development-with-rails/hartl-michael/products_products/detail/prod_id/64776954/

McGraw, G. (2006). *Software Security: Building Security In.* Addison-Wesley.

Howard, M., & Lipner, S. (2006). *The Security Development Lifecycle: SDL: A Process for Developing Demonstrably More Secure Software.* Microsoft Press.

OWASP. (2022). *OWASP Top Ten.*

ISO/IEC. (2022). *ISO/IEC 27001: Information Security Management.*

OWASP. (2022). *OWASP SAMM (Software Assurance Maturity Model).*

NIST. (2022). *NIST Special Publication 800-64 Rev. 2: Security Considerations in the System Development Life Cycle.*

SANS Institute. (2022). *Secure DevOps: A Practical Introduction.*

Microsoft. (2022). *DevOps for Security: Microsoft SDL and DevOps.*

www.ingramcontent.com/pod-product-compliance
Lightning Source LLC
LaVergne TN
LVHW080049210926
848481LV00011B/3307
* 9 7 9 8 9 9 0 7 2 0 9 0 9 *